Bright Child—
Poor Grades

Bright Child—
Poor Grades

THE PSYCHOLOGY OF UNDERACHIEVEMENT

by Barry Bricklin, Ph.D.
and Patricia M. Bricklin, Ph.D.

DELACORTE PRESS

Contents

4 3 8 0 8

Preface

An underachiever is a child whose day-by-day efficiency in school (and elsewhere) is much poorer than would be expected on the basis of his intelligence. A vast number of these children are underachieving because of conflicted emotional attitudes. This book is about such conflicts, and suggests ways of bringing about positive change. It also covers other, not directly "psychological" causes; for example, the teacher who picks on the child, the neighborhood that devalues education, failure in one particular subject which spreads to other subjects, the bright but bored child, and many others. Positive recommendations are made to combat these causes.

Primary concern is not with the brain-damaged child but rather the emotionally conflicted child who works inefficiently (or not at all). This child is found under various labels: disinterested, lazy, negative, unmotivated, uncooperative, "late bloomer," inattentive, daydreamer, and so forth.

These labels fail to convey the real reason for the lack of work. Most frequently the "lazy" child is psychologically *unable* to work efficiently and has no more conscious control over his "laziness" than he would over the course of a cold. In some few instances the "lazy" child may have patterned himself after a passive parent. In this case, the laziness is not caused by conflict. The child had the unfortunate luck to imitate a nonambitious person. Laziness caused by emotional conflict is handled very differently from other forms.

The book also focuses on how to distinguish between underachievement which is temporary or "situational" from that which is chronic. Temporary underachievement will fade out with the passage of time or with a change in the child's situation, whereas chronic underachievement will not.

Children who happen to manifest underachieving patterns in reading are at a particular disadvantage, since reading is a basic tool subject, the proper functioning of which is required for achievement in other areas. Successful reading depends upon the coordinated functioning of a large number of even more basic skills, e.g., perceptual-motor, language, auditory and visual discrimination, etc. Effective reading is particularly vulnerable to difficulty, since such a vast number of areas is involved.

A highly trained reading expert is often required to determine the exact role reading factors are playing in a given case. When these factors are primary, special remedial reading techniques (which are not covered in this work) may be needed.

Anyone who writes a book like this is guided by some sort of implicit philosophy. We do not recommend trying to impress the child with the glories of driving ambition and/or overly perfectionistic work habits. To borrow a Zen outlook, our purpose is to increase the child's ability to pursue excellence by changing the psychological conditions under which he lives—from those which would demand compulsive perfection to those which yield freedom to join the academic game. This approach, then, does not merely produce an achieving child, but rather a child who achieves and is also reasonably happy.

Many persons have been of direct help in the preparation of this book. Dr. Morris Chalick and Dr. George Lasota, now psychiatrists, aided in a tremendous number of ways during their student days at Jefferson Medical College. Lewis Kirshner helped in many of the same ways, as did Mrs. Adele Schiro. All of the aforementioned administered tests, interviewed parents, and made stimulating comments.

The contributions of Dr. Zygmunt A. Piotrowski will be quite obvious after the first few chapters have been read and need no affirmation here.

Other persons have helped indirectly, by making either their data or their ideas available to us.

Mike Halbert, of the Market Science Institute, a tremendously gifted person intellectually, forces anybody with intellectual pretensions and pride either to think better or to avoid his company.

Edward R. Dubin, director of the Valley Day School for children with adjustment and learning problems, a keen thinker in these areas, cooperated in studying many of the children.

Dr. Ruth Stekert, an amazingly perceptive pediatrician, often spotted potential underachievers long before anyone else, and was of great help in evaluating these children.

Thanks are due to two gentlemen who made no direct contributions to this work, but whose general outlooks have been influential. They are Dr. Robert Waelder, professor of psychoanalysis at the Jefferson Medical College, and Dr. Van Buren O. Hammett, professor and chairman of Hahnemann Medical College's psychiatric department. Neither man will allow his sense of truth and good observation—whether these be applied to matters of profession or world—to be compromised by theoretical disposition.

We should also like to thank Miss Helen Matthews, director of the Matthews School, Dr. Roy Kress, director of the Temple University Reading Clinic, Dr. Marjorie Johnson, director of Temple University Reading Clinic's laboratory school, and Dr. Edward Wallerstein, psychiatrist, for help in shaping and molding some of our ideas—although we assume personal blame for any bad ones.

We are grateful to WCAU radio, the CBS station in Philadelphia. Their request that we do a daily program on child psychology encouraged us to rethink and sharpen many of our ideas. Nothing is more effective for forcing one to discard fuzzy ideas than having to give sensible answers to intelligent questions within a limited time, with a sizable group listening and evaluating. Especially helpful suggestions have come from Mike Grant, program manager, and Dan Curtis, our broadcast colleague.

Linda Haage and Gloria Lavenberg patiently went through numerous revisions of the presentation without undue complaint.

Finally, we should like to thank the children and parents with whom we have had the pleasure of working in the areas covered by this book.

Introduction

The number of people engaged in professional jobs increased 46 per cent during the 1950s. The trend will continue. Modern methods and machinery grow ever more complex. The people who run these systems will have to possess complex skills. There can be no doubt that education and good work in school will play increasingly important roles in our lives and especially in the lives of our children.

Our interest in education extends, we hope, beyond salary and "prestige." All of us should want our children to express and use the best that is in them. Intellectual talent is an important resource of our country and of the world. It is a scarce resource.

Many potentially bright children have been denied an education in the past because they appeared stupid in class. These children were not identified as underachievers; they were labeled "stupid" and excluded from class. We lacked psychological tests to identify and understand these potentially bright children.

Some parents object to the new focus on education and individual testing. Many have said to us: "What is all this new-fangled stuff about tests and underachievement? We had none of that in my day." These parents are right. In "their day" any child who could not keep up with his class was eventually excluded. Many of these children quit school to take low-level jobs. Others simply dropped out, to spend many years "drifting." These children failed to obtain adequate educations. No one knew how to recognize the underachiever.

Today we recognize the seriousness and wide extent of underachievement. Here are some instructive figures to consider.

Anywhere from 15 to 40 per cent of *all* school children are underachievers. More than 60 per cent of the young adults who enter college do not finish. From our own data, we would estimate that almost one-half of all school children are not working up to, or even near, their potential intellectual levels.

In previous years no distinction was made between *potential* ability and *usable* ability. Potential ability refers to the level at which a child could work if he were free of debilitating emotional conflicts and tensions. Usable ability, sometimes called "functioning efficiency," refers to the level at which the child actually does work. Since measurement techniques were undeveloped, very little was made of the distinction between potential and actual performance. For this reason, the figures from earlier decades tend to underestimate the number of underachievers. The current emphasis on individual testing has given a more correct picture of the true extent of underachievement. In a recent investigation by the authors, 66 per cent of the male children with at least average intelligence in an eighth grade class had readily discernible reading problems. This number probably represents the true state of affairs in our schools.

Causes of underachievement fall into four categories. There are physical causes, such as poor vision or hearing. There are pedagogic or "teaching method" causes, such as when a child fails to learn because he is being taught poorly. There are sociological causes, such as when a child turns from school work because his peers and neighbors devalue education. And then there are emotional causes, where the child does poorly because of emotionally conflicted attitudes. Our data suggest that at least 80 per cent of all underachievers are doing poorly because of emotional tensions. Most of the so-called chronic underachievers —intelligent boys and girls (mostly boys)—do poor work because they suffer from debilitating conflicts.

This book is concerned with children in the latter category. Even in cases where emotional conflict is not the primary cause of poor work, it still plays a major role. A child's realization that he is doing poorly produces emotional tension. This tension lowers his confidence. And so what may begin as an educational problem on the basis of some factor other than emotional conflict is *sustained* as a problem because of emotional conflict.

Many fruitless hours have been spent in professional circles arguing about which comes first: the educational problem or the emotional problem. The verdict of one camp is that the frustration that results from poor school work produces the child's tension; therefore the educational problem is basic. "Ridiculous," says the opposing side. "The child would not have done poorly to begin with if he did not have a conflict."

Both sides, of course, may be correct. Some bright children do seem to develop educational problems in the absence of psychological conflict. In many such cases—where the problem developed in the absence of significant tensions—the problem is *sustained* as a problem on the basis of ever-increasing emotional pressure. Our approach is pragmatic: break the cycle at the most efficient point. This may involve tutoring the child, parental counseling, psychotherapy, all of these measures—or none.

Much of the authors' work with underachieving children has involved diagnostic psychological and educational testing. After all the tests have been administered and studied, it is customary to hold a conference with the parents. The test results are discussed in these conferences, along with our recommendations for positive action. Many parents have told us that if they had had this information in the past, underachievement patterns could have been avoided. This book is an invitation to attend such a postdiagnostic conference, albeit a more extended and complete one than would be possible to hold for any single case.

Special Note to Parents

You will notice that the book is divided into two main parts. Part I spells out the psychological causes of underachievement; Part II is concerned with positive recommendations. An understanding gained from the material in Part I will be more helpful than an uncritical application of the suggestions in Part II. This book aims to *change attitudes*. Changes in significant parental attitudes will increase the child's efficiency. Part I will show which attitudes need to be changed, and furnish the understanding that must come before such change is possible. The causes have been separated from the recommendations to stress the importance of understanding the causes. Most parents want to begin "doing something" before they understand what is really going on. The positive recommendations in Part II do indeed suggest concrete actions, but if the changed outlook pointed to by Part I is absent, these actions will have minimal effect.

Introductory Notes to the
Professional Reader

This book emerged from a long-term follow-up investigation of children who had taken batteries of psychological tests. These children and their parents were contacted a number of years after the children had taken the tests in order to obtain information about their ongoing lives. The initial test data were compared with certain aspects of the eventual follow-up conditions. Our purpose was to isolate test elements of prognostic importance.

The children had been tested for a variety of reasons. The number of children referred to us because of school underachievement was tremendous. This fact, plus some others which occurred to us as we worked with underachieving children both in educational and in psychotherapeutic situations, compelled us to write this book. We were concerned not only about the large number of underachievers but also about the fact that chronic underachieving patterns are resistant to change, both educationally and psychologically. In all treatment-oriented disciplines, prevention is of prime importance. Nowhere is this more evident than in the area of underachievement. It is far easier to prevent a child from doing poorly in school than it is to improve his work once his grades have been consistently low. The best place to initiate a preventive program is in the home.

Most psychotherapists agree it is no easy matter to "cure" or change the emotional patterns of chronic underachievers. It is difficult to get good therapeutic results with many underachievers —even with those who otherwise do not seem "disturbed." Many an underachiever enters the psychotherapist's office, sits down, chats, is pleasant, cooperates at a superficial level, and leaves cordially at the end of the session. He returns for his next session and the same thing occurs. This may happen regardless of the therapeutic approach employed.

Of course results are not always discouraging. There are always the dramatic successes. But the number of underachievers who can be helped within a *reasonable* length of time and at a *reasonable* cost is still too small.

The underachiever is often perplexing to work with. He may seem calm and unruffled on the surface. It is often difficult to initiate pertinent topics for discussion during the therapeutic hour, and the typical underachiever has a hard time in seeing any connection between his emotional life and the quality of his school work. Therapeutic passivity is only successful in a small number of cases. Since the typical underachiever has a passive-aggressive personality, this poses quite an obstacle to fruitful results. Our point, again, is that prevention is an easier proposition than remediation.

Although what the parents of underachievers "do" to their children are functions of deeply ingrained personality patterns, it is possible to substantially ameliorate the "pathology" with insight.

We believe the psychological conditions described in this book account for the majority of cases of underachievement. Subsequently, we believe that a positive change in these conditions will lead to a significant reduction in the number of cases of underachievement. We feel that if parents can be made to see and to understand the things they do that engender or sustain patterns of underachievement, these patterns can be significantly changed.

Some of the conclusions cited in this book were derived from the long-term follow-up study mentioned before. Other conclusions have been derived from the authors' own individual work with these children. This work has involved psychological and educational diagnosis, educational tutoring, classroom teaching, and psychotherapy.

Rorschach Data on an Underachieving Group and Two Control Groups

We would like to present to our professional audience part of the data from which some of these conclusions have been drawn.

Among the test data on the followed-up children were Rorschach data. (All of the technical data and conclusions of this follow-up study are being prepared for separate presentation.)

Dr. Zygmunt A. Piotrowski (*Perceptanalysis*, New York: Macmillan, 1957) has elucidated the importance of the Human Movement response, first pointed to by Hermann Rorschach (in *Psychodiagnostik*, second edition, Bern and Berlin: Huber, 1932). Dr. Piotrowski demonstrated that the M response (M is the abbreviation for the Human Movement response) reflects an interpersonal attitude. A Rorschach Human Movement, or M, response would be: "Two people dancing," or "A person lifting his arms," that is, an organism, usually human, in a human muscular attitude. An interpersonal attitude is a complex tendency to feel, think, and act in a certain definite manner in an interpersonal situation which subjectively has at least some potentially important consequences. This manner of thinking, acting, and feeling can be inferred from the kinesthetic elements of the M responses. Although M responses come in a wide variety of kinesthetic types (they come in as many "types" as a person can think, feel, and act in interpersonal situations as reflected by an almost endless variety of kinesthetic attitudes), it is possible to classify them in the following manner.

An aggressive M refers to a response in which the primary kinesthetic attitude is aggressive, such as "Two people fighting." This type of kinesthetic response reflects a tendency to adopt an aggressive attitude in certain life situations. By the manner in which the M appears in the total sequence of responses, and by evaluating the blot area upon which the M is projected, it is possible to ascertain which life area or psychological environment is likely to elicit this particular interpersonal attitude. For example, an aggressive M given to plate IV would suggest that the testee has a tendency to feel most (not exclusively) aggressively inclined in interaction with male authority figures. (The ability to predict the environment most likely to elicit the action tendency by means of the particular plate responded to is disputed by some professional Rorschach workers.) If this M is also a W, or whole, response, that is, if the projected image encompasses the entire area of plate IV, the testee reveals a greater readiness to activate the aggressive action than would be true had the image encompassed but a small detail of the plate. There is no space here to present Piotrowski's brilliantly thought-out perceptanalytic system, but we do want to show how it is possible to isolate and identify major interpersonal attitudes and to set forth some of the pertinent aspects of their eliciting conditions.

As we see then, M responses may be aggressive. An aggressive M indicates an aggressive inclination (with an intensity greater than "normal") in certain interpersonal situations. M may also be assertive, compliant, submissive, etc., depending upon the predominant kinesthetic attitude "seen." In general, if the projected human figure gives in to the force of gravity, a compliant or submissive interpersonal attitude is revealed (depending on the degree of "giving in"). If the figure overcomes the force of gravity, an assertive attitude is indicated. A compliant interpersonal attitude reflects a tendency to seek out other people to assume final responsibilities (or "justifications") for important interpersonal actions and decisions. An assertive interpersonal attitude reveals a tendency to assume personal responsibility—to "locate" the source of personal evaluation within one's own personality (and not in some external source, such as a parent, boss, public opinion, etc.). An assertive M would be: "Two people dancing." The kinesthetic attitude in this response, dancing, is assertive, and hence the interpersonal attitude reflected is one of assertiveness. Sometimes the predominant kinesthetic attitude is one of limited assertiveness, such as "A person talking." There is no complete overcoming of the force of gravity here; the attitude is rather one of limited assertiveness. A compliant M would be "A person sitting down"—the kinesthetic attitude one of giving in to the force of gravity. The reflected interpersonal attitude is hence one of compliance—a tendency to seek out others, or allow others, to have ultimate responsibility. "A person lying down" would be a submissive M. This is a complete "giving in" to the force of gravity.

A subject may see a figure in danger, such as "A man about to fall over a cliff." This reflects insecurity and fear in certain situations. We classify such responses as "M danger." The figures may be seen as exerting energy but to no avail, such as: "Two figures in a tug of war with neither person winning." This type of response, usually produced by obsessives, is termed "blocked." Mental energy is exerted, but no decisions or decisive actions are being made. When the kinesthetic attitude is projected onto a very weak, nonexistent, noncorporeal body, such as a ghost or genie, the response is scored "M weakness." There is little "push" behind attitudes thus projected.

The categories of M types used in Table 1 are: aggressive M projected onto tiny detail areas; aggressive M projected onto other than small detail areas; assertive M (any area); limited assertive M (any area); compliant M (any area); submissive M (any area); M seen in ghosts or genies, called "weakness" (any area); and M blocked (any area).

Table 1 shows by type the mean number of Human Movement responses produced by ninety children: a group of forty under-achieving youngsters, a group of twenty-five exceptionally well achieving children, and a group of twenty-five children with

TABLE 1

*The Mean Number of Responses in Certain Human Movement
Categories in an Underachieving Group, an Achieving Group,
and a Group with Miscellaneous Emotional Conflicts.*

	I Under-achievers (N = 40)	II Achievers (N = 25)	III Other Conflict (N = 25)	Signif. Diff.
Aggressive, detail	1.4	.2	.3	I—II,III
Aggressive, other	.2	.2	2.0	I,II—III
Assertive	.4	2.8	.8	I,III—II
Limited Assertive	1.8	2.0	1.4	none
Compliant	.8	.8	1.0	none
Submissive	—	—	.8	I,II—III
Danger	.6	—	.6	I,III—II
Weakness	.4	—	—	I—II,III
Blocked	.2	—	.4	I,III—II
Mean Number of M	5.8	6.0	7.3	

other types of emotional conflicts. Ages ranged between eight and
sixteen. The children in the underachieving group took part in
the long-term follow-up study. None of this group had any other
striking "overt" problems; underachievement was the sole, readily
identifiable "disturbance." The children in the high achievement
group did not take part in the follow-up study. These children
were bright and well-functioning, sustaining the equivalent of
a B or better average in major subjects. They were selected from
among cases who had been tested for vocational reasons (seven
cases), and from among control cases originally gathered for another purpose. The group with other types of emotional conflicts
is composed of members whose primary problems did not involve
underachievement. In some few cases underachievement was part
of the total clinical picture, but the underachievement in these
cases was clearly secondary to a more serious neurotic or acting-
out disturbance. This group will be referred to as the "Other
Conflict" group. Age and intelligence were not significantly different among the three groups.

The fourth, or "Signif. Diff.," column in Table 1 shows which groups differed in which areas. For example, the top entry under the fourth column shows the following: Group I, the Under-achievers, earned a mean score in aggressive M projected onto small detail areas that was different from the mean scores earned by the Achievers group, II, and by the Other Conflict group, III. This is indicated by the dash separating I from II and III. To show that the mean scores in small-detail aggressive M were not different between groups II and III, a comma was used instead of a dash. Coincidently, in no score area were *all* three groups significantly different from one another (which would have been indicated by I—II—III had it occurred).

Now look at the first two rows across. These data suggested one of the main conclusions cited in this book, one suspected to be true for a long time but heretofore validated in only a few instances. These data clearly indicate that most underachievers are characterized by passive-aggressive orientations. The Under-achievers produced 1.4 small-detail aggressive M responses on the average, while the Achievers and the Other Conflict group members produced .2 and .3 respectively. In other words, the underachievers are characterized by a tendency to feel very angry (aggressive M kinesthesias in many responses). But at the same time they feel safe in expressing this anger only in limited areas of life (little detail responses). This is confirmation of the passive-aggressive hypothesis. The majority of underachievers are hyper-aggressively inclined but can only express this aggressiveness in limited life areas. (Some remarks are made later on the differ-ences between aggression, anger, hostility, etc.) There is no "total ego" involvement in the aggressiveness of the underachiever. Compare this to the Other Conflict group. This group produced more aggressive kinesthesias in total (row one + row two, i.e., .3 + 2.0 = 2.3) than the Underachieving group (1.4 + .2 = 1.6), but the Other Conflict group expresses more aggressiveness in "open" areas (their aggressive responses were not confined to small-detail areas). It is interesting that both the Underachiever and the Other Conflict groups produced more aggressive M in total than did the Achievers. The Other Conflict group produced 2.3, the Underachiever group 1.6, and the Achiever group .4. Only the Underachievers, however, projected the substantial majority of their aggressive responses onto small-detail areas.

The members of the Underachiever group and the Other Conflict group reflect more frustration than do the members of the Achiever group (more aggressive responses in total). The Underachiever often feels angry, but the anger is not consciously acceptable (aggressive responses limited to small-detail areas). This finding is underscored in Table 2. Thirty-one of the forty Under-

TABLE 2

*Aggressive Human Movement Responses
Seen in Small-Detail Areas
for Underachieving, Achieving, and Other Conflict Groups*

	At least 1	None	Total
Underachievers	31	9	40
Other Conflict	6	19	25
Achievers	4	21	25
	41	49	90

Chi Square $= 28.16$; $P < .001$

achievers produced at least one aggressive M that was limited to a small-detail area. The low mean-value figure of 1.4 for aggressive M projected onto small details by the Underachievers might have belied this fact. But Table 2 shows that fully *31 of the 40* Underachievers produced an aggressive M projected onto a small-detail area. Three of the 9 Underachieving cases who failed to produce small-detail aggressive M responses produced no M at all. Only 4 of the Achievers, and 6 of the Other Conflict members produced small-detail aggressive M.

Table 3 shows the number in each of the three groups who produced what we call aggression-directed-at-organism-in-the-past responses. These are exemplified by responses such as:

"A tiger. They killed him and used him for a rug."

"A foot cut off. Just laying there."

"A butterfly that had been hit—smashed."

"A tail—taken off."

"A bear. He's been cut in half."

TABLE 3

Aggression-Directed-at-Organism-in-the-Past Responses,
for Underachieving, Achieving, and Other Conflict Groups

	At least 1	None	Total
Underachievers	29	11	40
Other Conflict	7	18	25
Achievers	1	24	25
	37	53	90

Chi Square $= 46.12$; $P < .001$

"A branch. Dead. Broken off."

"A leg chopped off."

"The legs have been damaged—blood."

"The whole part of the face has been blown away."

"The hands have been broken. They want to get away from each other."

"A bone—broken off."

As may be noted, these responses reflect a fear of aggressive retaliation (psychoanalysts call this castration anxiety). The interesting thing is that in each instance the aggressive action is projected into the past. (The analysts might say that many of these cases have accepted the "fact" of psychological demasculinization.) From one standpoint, we are interested that the aggressive act is projected "away" from the ego. We interpret this to mean the underachiever has a heightened fear of his own anger, of ensuing aggressive retaliation from others, and of the possible destruction of his love or dependency objects and subsequently of himself. Another way of saying this is that the underachiever is overly frightened by the feeling of anger. He fears his own anger and the anger of others to excessive degrees. Just as he projects aggressive attitudes into small-detail areas, he projects anger and hostility into the past, "away" from the ego.

Angry feelings are definitely unacceptable to the underachiever. The responses called "aggression directed at organism in the past" reflect simultaneously unacceptable anger and a dread fear of retaliation.

These facts are clear. The Other Conflict group members, composed of neurotic and acting-out children, and the Underachievers have a larger amount of aggressive attitudes than the Achievers (Table 1). But the aggressiveness is much less acceptable to the Underachievers than to the members of the other two groups (Tables 1, 2, 3).

Let us, for a moment, return to Table 1. The Underachievers produced only .4 assertive M responses on the average, while this same value was 2.8 for the Achievers, and .8 for the Other Conflict group. A typical achiever clearly has a greater sense of personal inner freedom and can act more on his own initiative and can better accept personal responsibility than can the Underachiever, or the neurotic, or the child with poor self-control.

All groups produced roughly the same number of compliant responses. The average member of the achieving group does not mind leaning on others at times. The action tendencies revealed in M are not mutually exclusive. The presence of compliant M, or compliant attitudes, for example, does not rule out the possibility of assertive behavior. The two tendencies are not mutually exclusive. A person's record may show predominately assertive M with, say, one compliant M. This means that the testee is assertive in most life situations, but in at least one area would not mind seeking direction from someone else.

The Underachiever and the Other Conflict group members produced more M danger than did the achievers, and more M blocked. These children feel themselves to be in more precarious situations than the Achievers. There is, further, less of a tendency to obsessive rumination among the Achievers.

Piotrowski has shown that the Whole response (W) is a measure of the degree to which an individual will exert himself toward the accomplishment of goals for which society bestows reward, praise, and recognition. The W response, in one carefully defined sense, may thus be indicative of ambitiousness. The relationship between W and the apparent clinical equivalents of W (e.g., ambitiousness, tendency to work hard) is often a complicated one. Our test(s) have shown that more underachievers have few W's than have achievers, but there are some underachievers who have many W's. What is interesting is the fact so many underachievers produced what we have termed comment-on-whole-difficulty-or-ease. This type of comment bespeaks a feeling of anxious frustration in the area of ambition and achievement. An individual who produces this type of comment wants to "produce," but is afraid and inhibited. The following are examples:

"I'm not sure what the whole thing could be."

"It's hard to make anything out of this" (it being clearly implied that "this" is the whole card).

"Ah, this looks like one whole thing" (accompanied by a relieved tone).

"I don't know what the whole thing could be."

"This is *definitely* a bat [to the whole of a plate]; I'm sure of this one."

These "comments" indicate a fear of tackling the W task. The differences in this area among the three groups were striking, as a glance at Table 4 will prove. This table tells an interesting story

TABLE 4

*Comment-on-Whole-Difficulty-or-Ease
in Underachieving, Achieving, and Other Conflict Groups*

	At least 1	None	Total
Underachievers	27	13	40
Other Conflict	7	18	25
Achievers	2	23	25
	36	54	90

Chi Square $= 24.77$; $P < .001$

when it is combined with the following fact: Both the achievers and the underachievers produced many so-called unrealistic syntheses. An unrealistic synthesis occurs when two areas of a blot are inappropriately joined to form one response, e.g. (to Plate V), "A bat with human legs." (This is not as serious as a genuine perceptual fusion—the so-called contaminations.) An unrealistic synthesis occurs when the testee is so intent on giving organization to the blot that he unrealistically synthesizes the various blot elements into one response, even when the various elements are not realistically adjoined. Another example would be (to Plate VI):

"That looks like an animal hide on the bottom there, and it looks like a horse's foot coming out of the top." The two major elements of this response would have been more appropriately seen separately.

A nonpsychotic person who produces unrealistic syntheses has a strong inclination to organize and integrate his experiences, but in some instances the desire to "organize" outstrips the capacity. (In psychotics, unrealistic syntheses are more often the result of poor critical self-control.) In normals the unrealistic synthesis is designed to integrate and render control. The underlying motivations among nonpsychotics may not always be identical; e.g., some do this because of a defensive fear of aggression, others because they fear a lack of self-control, others because of too much ambition, and so forth. The unrealistic synthesis is always more serious in the adult's record than in the child's.

It is interesting that both the Achievers (16 cases) and the Underachievers (23 cases) produced unrealistic syntheses. Underachievers and achievers are highly interested in integration—in doing well. The members of both groups have a "W compulsion," in this sense. However, as Table 4 shows, this desire is accompanied by few "comments" in the achieving group, showing a lack of frustration, but with many "comments" in the underachieving group, reflecting frustration and fear.

To summarize, the achievers and the underachievers do not differ markedly in the total number of Whole responses produced (the mean values would be misleading, since variability is high in both groups). Both underachievers and achievers produce far more unrealistic syntheses then do other children (no more than 10 per cent of cases would produce this sign in a randomly selected group of children). Consequently, the members of *both* groups are interested in good achievement—*overly* interested for that matter. However, where the two groups differ is in the production of comments-on-whole-difficulty-or-ease. And so while both groups *desire* to achieve, the members of the underachieving group fall short of the goal—afraid to tackle the "W job." This means that although the underachiever is clearly impelled to go after the W, he is afraid he might fail at the job. It was clear in the performances of the underachievers that they felt notably relieved when they could get an "easy" (Plate V) or "definite" W: "This is *definitely* a bat; I'm sure of this one." These data strongly indicate that the underachiever's sense of security is at stake when he tries for a W. He is afraid he might fail. This is taken to reflect the fact that the underachiever has overly linked his sense of self worth to his ability to accomplish. The underachiever wants to accomplish —he wants to very badly (many unrealistic syntheses)—but he is afraid to risk failure (many "comments"). This is one of the themes of the work to follow.

PART ONE

The Psychological Causes
of Underachievement

1

The Underachieving Child: Who He Is
and How to Spot Him

Two underachieving youngsters, accompanied by their mothers, sit in the psychologist's waiting room. They are quiet and uncomfortable. Both are boys. This is not surprising: 80 per cent of children with educational problems are boys.

Both are eleven years old and in the sixth grade. They are well dressed. Each boy looks alert and "intelligent," yet is having trouble with his sixth grade work. Each mother realizes that soon her child will enter junior high school, and has known for some time that her child was having trouble in school. In one child's case the poor work extended to all subjects; in the other child's case, it started with trouble in one subject and spread. And yet both mothers postponed definite action. Even as they sit in the waiting room they wonder if they are doing the right thing. They ask themselves: "Would he grow out of it anyway?" "Is it a mistake to make him feel different?" "Where have I failed?"

Meanwhile, the boys are frightened, annoyed, and embarrassed —but hate to admit these things, even to themselves.

Parents usually think an educational problem exists when the child's grades slip. In some instances, a teacher may report the child's work is not in keeping with what is considered his true ability. Each of these sources of information—low grades or an estimation by the teacher, unsupported by test data—should be considered only as points of departure in the diagnoses of educational problems. School grades do not take into account the child's potential capacities. Teacher's estimations are often biased by a child's physical appearance and by the degree to which he cooperates in class. Studies show that teachers tend to see cooperative, well-behaved children as more intelligent and as better students than poorly behaved children. This is not a criticism of the teacher. No person can know accurately what goes on "inside" a child by gross observation alone. Meanwhile, most classrooms are overcrowded—a condition which makes it increasingly difficult for teachers to offer individual attention.

The scientific approach to poor school work proceeds by seeking the answers to five questions. We will discuss these questions in the order in which the psychologist would ask them of himself.

1. *What can be expected of the child from the standpoint of general capacity for learning?*

Before we can answer any question about an educational problem, we must determine the child's general *potential* capacity for learning. In other words, we ask: If this child were free from tension, had good self-confidence, and had reasonably good teachers, how well could we expect him to do in school? Unless there is a significant gap between his potential ability and his current functioning ability, we are not justified in talking about an educational "problem"—no matter what his grades happen to be. For if the child has a mediocre potential capacity for learning, mediocre school grades would be expected. This does *not* mean that the parents should give up on providing the best possible education for a "mediocre" child; it does mean that the child is not an underachiever.

How is it possible to gain some idea of a person's potential? The answer is: by an inspection of certain aspects of his performance in a variety of tests, especially in certain *sections* of an intelligence test. But *a person's potential capacity is not known by a simple I.Q. value.* The Intelligence Quotient is a number that conveniently summarizes general functioning ability in a wide variety of tasks. The actual value indicates how an individual functions in these tasks compared to other persons his age. Hence the I.Q. is essentially a comparative number. It is useful because we can predict a wide range of behaviors with it, and because it is relatively stable over time. An I.Q. varies little unless the child is exposed to very unusual or exceptional conditions. However, it is not true that an I.Q. "never" changes. If a child is moved from a dull, passive, and nonalert environment to a bright, active, inquisitive environment, his I.Q. may change, especially if this occurs when he is young. And why not? That behavior of the child, which we see as reflecting intelligence, will have changed. The I.Q. accurately reflects a person's functioning efficiency at certain tasks under a wide variety of conditions. The I.Q. helps us plan an educational program that is suited to individual needs. A person is not given an I.Q. label and "damned to it"—at least not by professionally trained users, who realize its usefulness but are aware of its limitations and of its correct interpretation.

Some recently published articles have sought to impress upon the public the "evil" of the I.Q., in that it may damn a child to a nonproductive life. These articles are usually written by ill-informed, sensation-seeking individuals. It is true, however, that some people use the I.Q. incorrectly. Some lack sufficient training, but this is not the test's fault. Universities and colleges are aware of this occasional abuse of the I.Q. So are the companies who publish the tests. They are all actively concerned with eliminating the misuse of intelligence tests.

The I.Q. is a summary number. It is an "average." As such, the single I.Q. value does not accurately gauge potentialities.

The trained evaluator, a psychologist in this instance, first inspects the child's performance on certain parts of the intelligence test. Certain abilities, like general reasoning and the capacity to abstract general ideas from specific instances, are not affected by emotional tension to the same degree as are some other intellectual abilities, such as immediate attention span. So the child's comparative performances in these areas furnish approximations of his potential abilities.

The psychologist will not be impressed with mere quantitative scores alone, but will pay attention to the quality of performance. Two answers to a problem may both be right, but one could show a higher degree of creativeness and inventiveness. On the personality tests, he will inspect the range and breadth of interests, the ease of associative ability, and so on. By inspecting the child's performance on a wide variety of tasks—tasks not affected significantly by tension—we gain an idea of potential intellectual ability and of how the child would do if he were free of excessive tension.

2. *What is the child's day-by-day functioning ability—how is the child actually doing?*

At first we asked, How well *can* he perform? Now we ask, How *does* he perform? This question can be answered with other areas of the intelligence test as well as by achievement tests, interview data, and school grades, to some extent. When there is a gap between these two major areas, what the child could do and what he does do, we are justified in talking about underachievement.

These are the areas in which the clinician seeks the answer:

a) The child's storehouse of general facts and information. What facts has the child actually acquired to date?

b) The child's actual reading ability. Here we are interested in more than the child's ability to pronounce words. (Many parents tend to identify reading with "reading aloud"—a rather serious error.) Under "reading" we are interested in all of the following: the child's ability to recognize and pronounce words; the number of words the child can define; his ability to "attack" words, that is, to apply the rules of phonics; his comprehension of the material read, including both factual content as well as inferential content (that which "goes beyond" the material); his ability to organize the material meaningfully; his ability to criticize and evaluate what he reads. In general, the psychologist is interested in total language development. Aside from reading, we are interested in the child's speaking abilities and his writing abilities. These may also be measured.

c) We may measure the child's achievement in specialized areas, such as arithmetic, social studies, sciences, etc.

After the data is gathered, the psychologist compares the answer he obtained to question one (What can be expected?) to the answer obtained to question two (How is the child actually doing?). This provides the answer to the basic question:

3. *Is the child an underachiever?*

If the child is not accomplishing at a level commensurate with his intellectual ability, he is an underachiever. If a child is actually accomplishing at a level higher than would be expected (this has never happened to us; it is only likely to happen if the potential intellectual level is gauged from a single I.Q. value), the child is *not* labeled an "overachiever." We would surmise that should this happen, the clinician has estimated the potential level on an equivocal basis. There is the further possibility that a dull child may have fantastic motivation and diligence. (It is possible for a child to be a "compulsive" achiever. This is a child whose interest in achievement is based on a neurotically compulsive command for perfection and endless toil. However, the concept of overachiever as the opposite of underachiever makes no sense.)

In this system, even a child with reasonably good grades may be an underachiever. Say a child receives mostly C's and an occasional D on his report, but say this child has superior potential intelligence. His parents may be satisfied with his C grades. The child may be satisfied. This is certainly their right. However, the child would be an underachiever according to our system. One could argue that C grades are "acceptable," but this is another matter. A child who is not doing work commensurate with his potential capacity may quite reasonably be called an underachiever. On the other hand, consider the child who is receiving mainly D's. If this child has low potential capacity, he would not be an underachiever. This does not mean the parents could not try to raise the child's over-all effectiveness. It *does* mean we would *not* classify the child as an underachiever. In general, children who have superior potential intellectual ability should be able to earn A's and B's, with maybe an occasional C or even D. Children with high average intelligence should reasonably be able to maintain a B average, with perhaps occasional lapses. Children with average intelligence should be able to maintain a C average. The label "underachiever" is only used when the underachievement has been chronic (at least a full term's duration). The clinician rarely sees a case until the underachievement has been of a long term nature.

If the youngster is an underachiever, the next question is:

4. *What are the major contributing factors which account for the difference between his potential or expected ability, and his actual day-by-day accomplishment?*

There are four broad areas the psychologist will investigate as he seeks to find out why the child is an underachiever. They are:

a) Psychological factors: personal adjustment, etc.

b) Physiological factors: vision, hearing, etc.

c) Sociological factors: type of neighborhood, etc.

d) Pedagogical factors: teaching methods, etc.

Various investigators have estimated that from 40 to 90 per cent of the cases of underachievement are caused by emotional conflict. Our own data would indicate that the 90 per cent figure is probably correct.

Any child who is suspected of being a chronic underachiever should in addition to seeing a psychiatrist see a physician, who may recommend other specialists (if indicated). Some educational clinics have equipment to do vision and hearing screening tests. Physiological factors account for an exceedingly small number of underachieving cases. Nevertheless, the evaluation should include the following areas: vision, hearing, glandular system, general health, and more specific neurologic functions, if indicated. The family physician, aided by the clinical psychologist in some instances, will decide if specific neurological tests are indicated.

The psychologist will investigate another area, the sociological one. Sociological factors include such things as the type of neighborhood in which the child lives, the emphasis placed on education around the home, and so forth. Some neighborhoods place a low value on education. A child who is interested in education is dubbed a sissy or worse in such neighborhoods. The bright child is often at a distinct disadvantage in such an environment.

Another area that needs investigation is the pedagogical, that is, teaching methods. Sometimes a child is being taught by means or methods that are not suited to him. Once in a while a child will be assigned to a badly overcrowded class. Surprisingly, we do not encounter many cases of underachievement caused *primarily* by these factors.

5. *How, for this particular child, can the gap between potential capacity and actual achievement best be closed?*

If the basic causes of the underachievement are physiological, the recommendations are obvious. If glasses are needed, the child should get glasses; if the child has a hearing loss, it should be corrected, and so on.

If the primary cause is sociological—say the neighborhood attitude is that good school work is for "grinds"—it is more difficult to take realistic action, but some suggestions are offered later.

If the basic cause of the underachievement is that the child has been taught with incorrect or unsuitable methods, the reading expert or the educational expert should plan a more optimal educational program.

The overwhelming odds are that the psychologist will find emotional conflict to be the prime cause of the underachievement. Quite commonly the psychologist will recommend a program consisting of improved psychological conditions around the home, and educational tutoring. If the problem is chronic and the child is already far behind in his school work, psychotherapy will probably be recommended as well. In very severe cases a special day or boarding school may be indicated.

The areas that need improvement in the child who is underachieving because of emotional conflict are his self-confidence, his study habits, and his fund of knowledge. Psychotherapy and improved home conditions "work on" the poor self-confidence. Tutoring, in the hands of a trained expert, preferably an individual who in addition to being a tutor is also a professional psychologist, "works on" the poor study habits and the poor fund of knowledge. Sometimes tutoring alone can serve to improve self-confidence as well as impart content. The child who is doing poor school work has a poor image of himself psychologically. Sometimes tutoring can improve his school work to a point where his image of himself becomes more positive, thereby increasing his self-confidence. When this happens, his school work will get even better—and his self image, in turn will get a further boost. In the more serious or chronic cases, a combined program of psychotherapy and tutoring is indicated.

After the test data have been gathered, and the causes of under-achievement have been determined, it is customary for the psychologist to have an interview with the child's parents. If it is a typical case, emotional conflict will have been found to play a large causal role. The psychologist will give the parents some suggestions. He will probably recommend some form of tutoring and may help plan this tutoring program. He will spend the larger part of the interview time telling the parents how to improve the psychological conditions around the house.

Let us return to the two boys we left in the waiting room. The boys are not being seen in a vacuum—they are the sum total of their life experiences. Both Bob and Fred are the youngest of four children. They were both described as healthy, active youngsters. Developmental histories were "average" in both cases. There were, however, two major differences in the early, preschool years.

Whereas *Bob's* early language development was quite normal, *Fred* was put under much parental pressure to speak excellently. Fred's parents would correct him each time a word was not pronounced with great clarity. Fred was taught that only perfection would be tolerated—and that nothing short of this was acceptable. He came to feel that he would be loved only if he were perfect. Whenever he became angry and expressed it, he was stifled by his parents—who would not tolerate anger. Fred now became afraid of the feeling of anger; he was afraid that his parents would become enraged and stop loving him if he were to act or even feel angry. During the second grade his work at school began to slip. Bob was doing satisfactory work at this point. Fred's work was "barely acceptable" during the first five grades. He was promoted because he managed to keep his work at a just-passing level. However, during the sixth grade year his self-confidence totally collapsed. For the first time he was doing failing work.

Bob, on the other hand, continued to do rather well in all subjects except arithmetic. As it turned out, he had not understood some of the fundamental rules of arithmetic and had not been given an adequate chance to ask proper questions at the proper time. As the years went on, he began to feel more and more insecure about everything that involved arithmetic. A strange but unfortunately common thing happened to Bob when he entered the sixth grade. His lack of confidence in himself, which was at first confined to arithmetic, spread to include other subjects. His self-confidence slipped to a point where all of his work suffered.

So in the sixth grade both Bob and Fred did poor work. On the intelligence test, both boys achieved superior I.Q. values (80 per cent of children who are underachievers have better than average intelligence).

But this was only part of the information revealed by the intelligence tests. Fred did very well on those items which reflect potential or expected capacity, but he did very poorly on those items which are most easily affected by emotional conflict and poor self-confidence. Fred also did poorly on the achievement tests. Personality tests revealed that Fred was incapable of maintaining a line of concentrated thought; the tests indicated further that he was resentful of the parental pressure he had been subjected to, but was afraid to express this resentment. The personality tests showed that due to poor self-confidence Fred could not pay attention or concentrate in class. They further showed that Fred was afraid of angry feelings. The psychologist recommended that Fred, and his parents as well, receive psychotherapy. The therapy was recommended for Fred so that he could be made to understand what forces had acted on him, why he had lost his self-confidence, and why his grades were poor. Psychotherapy in the form of weekly counseling sessions was necessary for the parents so they could be made to see and understand what they had been doing to their son. These neurotic patterns were so ingrained that the clinician decided a one-interview session would not be sufficient to show them what they were doing to Fred. In addition to the psychotherapy, Fred was also to receive tutoring—starting at a very basic level. Because of his early loss of confidence, Fred had been an inefficient learner from the very beginning. He needed tutoring in tool subjects, especially in reading. In addition, he had to be brought up to date on all the work he had missed during the first six years of school.

Bob also had superior potential or expected intellectual abilities. However, the results from those parts of the intelligence test that reflect day-by-day functioning ability were not especially low except for the portion that consisted of arithmetic items. Bob did very acceptable work on the achievement tests—even those which measure reading ability. This surprised the parents; they thought Bob's problem area was reading. As it turned out, Bob's temporary loss of self-confidence, based on his poor understanding of arithmetic, caused him to read poorly while he was in the school classroom. But he was not actually a poor reader. The achievement tests and the individual reading tests proved this. The personality tests revealed no significant conflicts. The psychologist's diagnosis of Bob was as follows: poor understanding of arithmetic, causing a temporary loss of self-confidence in all subjects. The psychologist recommended tutoring in arithmetic plus brush-up work in those subjects in which Bob had fallen temporarily behind. No psychotherapy was recommended, since Bob's loss of confidence was temporary and was not based upon a poor psychological environment in the home.

Bob was tutored in arithmetic and was "brushed-up" in other subjects. One year later he was doing acceptable work. At the time of this writing, Fred's work was starting to improve. He will likely be seen by a therapist for about two to two and a half years. The parents were seen for fifteen sessions each. If these parents had not waited so long before seeking professional help, these time periods could have perhaps been shortened.

Unfortunately, the number of "Freds" in the schools is large. The number of "Bobs" is much smaller.

Had Fred's parents known what they were doing, his problems

could have perhaps been avoided. This book is designed to offer that knowledge, and is an invitation to learn some of the things Fred's parents learned in their psychotherapeutic counseling sessions.

Keep in mind that when we speak about the underachiever, unless otherwise specified, we speak about the potentially bright child who is doing poor work because of underlying emotional conflict. These are the "neglected children" in our schools. They have much to contribute to society, but have been stifled in their efforts to do so.

2

An Overview: The Psychological Causes of Underachievement

No single underachiever will have all of the traits or conflicts mentioned in this work, and many times identical traits interact differently in different individuals. (We do not intend to become caught up here on the question of whether the term "trait" implies a "static" condition. Substitute the term "psychological process" if "trait" has such a connotation.)

The personality traits are considered in an order of diminishing frequency of appearance. The first trait considered, the passive-aggressive orientation, was found in a great majority of the under-achievers we studied. The next trait, an overlinkage between the sense of self worth and the ability to achieve, is likewise found with high frequency among underachievers. Almost all under-achievers are more concerned with avoiding failure than with achieving success.

One trait that dominates the personality of the underachiever is passive aggressiveness. The passive-aggressive person is terrified by the feeling of anger. Passive-aggressive children seek hidden ways to express anger, such as through the development of an education problem. Most passive-aggressive children are rather submissive and seemingly docile as far as overt behavior is concerned; they are rather pleasant to be with. However some few do express anger quite openly. Whether or not a particular passive-aggressive child happens to *act* aggressively or not (the majority do not), he nevertheless *fears the feeling* of anger. If in addition to being passive-aggressive, a given child should happen to have most of the other traits discussed, he is particularly likely to develop an educational problem. The passive-aggressive child with an educational problem strikes back at his parents where it "hurts"—in their pride over his achievement. He expresses his anger "passively" by wounding the parents' pride.

The underachiever typically equates his entire sense of self worth as an individual with his ability to achieve. He believes that his entire sense of worth "rides" on each and every little thing he may do. All of the little day-to-day things he must do in school, all of his exams—minor as well as major—assume to him an importance out of all proportion to reality. He tenses up when called upon to perform. This needless tension is one of the things that cause him to fail.

The vigorous pursuit of success is quite a different thing from a cautious and hampered retreat from possible failure. The underachiever is so afraid to be a failure in his own eyes that he does many strange things. Among the strangest things he may do is to refuse to study for exams or to take his work seriously. The underachiever tries to cling to the idea that he is "really" smart, but— and this is a crucial "but"—he fears putting this idea to the test. He would prefer not to study for an exam rather than study for it and perhaps *still* fail. And even more paradoxically, he ends up in the very state he tries so desperately to avoid.

Many underachievers are afraid to be anything but extraordinary. They dislike the idea of being "ordinary."

It is very strange, but many underachievers have a fear of success. Indeed, this is one of the amazing paradoxes of some underachievers. Very often two very different and "opposite" attitudes exist side by side within the personality of the underachiever. An individual who both fears success and failure is in a very difficult position.

Many underachievers psychologically overequate aggressive attitudes with competitive attitudes. Since most underachievers are already terrified by the idea of acting aggressively or even feeling angrily inclined, the idea of being competitive also becomes taboo. Because the underachiever psychologically sees competition as a form of aggression (and since angry feelings are taboo), he inhibits competitive attitudes. He inhibits them even in situations where they would be appropriate.

Underachievers have poor tolerance for frustration. They do not stay at a task very long. The typical underachiever will only try things he knows he can do. He must be assured success before he will even start.

Many underachievers have a marked tendency to regress. This means they deal with stress in infantile ways. They dislike personal responsibility.

Many underchievers will continue to do poor work in school even after they have been tutored and have obviously learned quite a bit of new material. Many are never able to demonstrate in the classroom the gains they have made during tutoring sessions.

Much has been written about the so-called overprotective mother. This is a rather poorly understood concept. The so-called overprotective mother is not actually overprotective most of the time; she is, in fact, most often in a rejecting, tense, and irritable frame of mind.

One interesting discovery in the field of juvenile delinquency is that some parents take secret pride in the defiant attitudes of their children. These parents (usually the father) wish they had the guts to be more pugnacious themselves. We occasionally find a bitter parent like this among the parents of underachievers. He sides with his child against the school and tries to blame the school for the child's poor work, when this attitude is unjustified. Even when a particular school or teacher is really to "blame" for a child's troubles, there are better ways of handling the situation than an open "siding" of the parents with a child "against" the school.

Many boys feel that school work is for sissies or for girls. A child who is already sensitive about his own masculinity may react very strongly to the fact that he is being asked to do school work. He inwardly feels he is being requested to do feminine work. Very often this child, who fears he may be inwardly weak, will be the most pugnacious and aggressive child in the classroom.

Some children are just plain "spoiled." These children are not used to having to exert themselves to accomplish anything. When school work gets too hard for them, they characteristically give up.

It would be unwise for the reader to skip the chapters on the causes of underachievement for the sake of going right to the recommendation chapters. We have no short-cut tricks for sale. We are offering a program that seeks to change the emotional attitudes around the house—attitudes which either foster or inhibit the child's learning capacities. Many parents know they do unwise or inhibiting things. They realize their tensions affect their children. And yet they cannot help themselves. A person cannot usually change his or her behavior in any meaningful way until he or she understands *why* the wrong things are being done. With understanding, change is possible. The purpose here is not to offer a list of do's and don'ts. It is to provide a degree of understanding that will improve the emotional climate of the home. The alert reader will see that *what is done* around the home is much less important than *the way things are done*. Actual overt behavior is less important than the accompanying emotional tones. *The goal of this work is to produce an emotional climate around the home that will help change an underachiever into an achiever.*

3.

Some Definitions of
Psychological Terms

One of the most widespread but least understood psychological terms is *unconscious,* which is used in many ways. When "Unconscious" is used in psychological circles, it almost never means a "loss of consciousness." "The unconscious" refers to complex processes, particularly those mental processes of which the individual has no awareness. Unconscious mental processes exert a very telling influence on a person's inner feelings and on his outer actions. These unconscious processes "contain" an individual's potential action tendencies, many of which if acted out or even experienced with full conscious clarity would bring psychological pain or grief to the individual. The activation or arousal of many of the potentials in the unconscious means "danger." When we say that a person is "unconscious" of something he does, we mean that he has no conscious awareness or understanding of the real reasons he is acting in that particular way. He may not even realize he is doing the thing in question. When psychologists speak about "real" reasons people do things, they mean reasons which are consistent with scientific theories of personality. They are entitled to speak of *real* reasons because when someone is brought to an awareness of these reasons he more readily will change his actual behavior and feelings. When a person is doing things that forever get him in difficulties or bring on psychological pain, the understanding and integration into the rest of the personality of these factors cause a change in his behavior.

Another word which will be used is *attitude.* An attitude is actually more complex psychologically than an opinion, although the two words are often used as though they mean the same thing. An opinion refers to a conscious idea—a verbal message or unit which "contains" what is believed about a certain thing. A person is conscious (aware) of his opinions. An attitude refers to a complex tendency to feel, act, and think in a certain manner. That is, an attitude consists of a muscular system response, and a tendency to behave in a certain definite way. An attitude of anger may cause the person's hair to stand on end, his fists and jaws to clench, his palms to sweat, and so forth. At the same time he may be thinking how much he would like to strike out at whatever he feels is causing the anger. At the very same time, but on another personality level, he may begin to fear the consequences of his action. An attitude contains a conscious "idea," an inner feeling, a definite reaction of the body, and also impulses and ideas which do not reach a conscious level. A person is *potentially* capable of verbalizing to himself and to others most of these component reactions, but will rarely do so with any clarity.

4.

The Passive-Aggressive Child

The passive-aggressive child would like to express current anger and stored-up resentments openly, but fears he may be punished or lose the love of his parents should he do so.* The term "passive" refers to the fact that the child typically does not

---

* Many authors and investigators object to the lack of precision in using words such as "anger," "aggression," and "hostility" as though they were interchangeable. Most theorists think of aggression as an inborn human reaction to frustration, its purpose being to help the organism overcome real or imagined frustrating obstacles. Some psychoanalysts insist the human being *must* "emit" aggression and that some form of frustration need not have evoked it. Such reasoning is usually based on pathologically extreme cases or on other theoretical issues not really related to aggression per se.

Hostility is usually seen as a form of aggression, its purpose being, at least on some level, to destroy a human being. Its use as a term generally implies a state of chronicity. It is unclear whether various authors intend the notion of "aggression" to imply these same properties. A recent trend is to distinguish between "constructive" and "destructive" aggression.

Although the term "anger" usually implies a clear conscious awareness of

express his angers openly but rather deviously or secretly, because he so fears what may happen to him if he expresses his angers and resentments openly. The child wishes to disguise angry intentions not only from his parents but also from himself. Part of his personality cannot tolerate feelings of anger, and so attempts to keep angry intentions from forming in his awareness and from being expressed. The child who is forever late, the bright person who persistently "botches" things, the child who constantly annoys his parents with demands for attention, the adult who "unwittingly" embarrasses his friends—all are passive-aggressive individuals. They do not consciously realize their displeasing behaviors are intended to express resentment and anger.

What originally starts as a fear of expressing anger openly, gradually becomes a fear of even feeling or experiencing angry intentions. At this point the child has lost his sense of inner freedom.

A person may have a passive-aggressive personality but still express anger openly on occasion. In fact, passive-aggressive children usually act in some extreme manner. The great majority are passive and docile in overt behavior, but some few act quite aggressively.

The passive-aggressive maneuver is sneaky aggressiveness. Passive-aggressive behavior obviously annoys whom it is intended to annoy, but the nonprofessional person would probably not think of calling this behavior "aggressive." The passive-aggressive

---

some feeling state (ranging from mild irritation to out-and-out rage), we have used the term in such a way that it is approximately interchangeable with aggression (where a clear subjective awareness of the aggressive state is *not* always assumed). This reflects our belief that the aggression being expressed by passive-aggressive individuals is so near the surface as to be readily discernible, even though it is often denied. After a period of successful psychotherapy the passive-aggressive person usually has no difficulty in seeing the anger behind his acts. "Anger" is also a term which makes more sense to a patient than "aggression."

We have made no systematic attempt to differentiate constructive and destructive aggression, even later when we speak of the relationship between aggression and competition. It is our impression that these concepts are dragged in at the last minute to label rather than explain behavior. One crucial area that must be understood to clarify these issues involves dependency and dependency conflict.

child hurts whom he intends to hurt, even though the hurt person and, in most cases, the child himself are not aware that resentment is being "expressed."

An underachiever *unconsciously* "knows" his poor school performance hurts parental pride. Most do not consciously realize their behavior is motivated by unacceptable feelings of anger.

The parents cannot tolerate genuine anger in their child. When he is young, they prevent him from expressing genuine anger and resentment. Even if they do not punish the child physically when he is angry, they communicate their extreme displeasure. Some parents of underachievers may *seemingly* not discourage the child from expressing anger. On the surface they may even seem to encourage the child to express anger. But they are inwardly frightened by anger. One mother of an underachiever told us she likes to see her child angry—that it makes her proud to see her boy "stand up for his rights." She would laugh and smile approvingly when the child "blew off steam." But later it became apparent that she really tolerated only phony anger, or anger not directed at her own person. When her little boy became angry at her, she panicked, and did everything she could to change his mood. She would fawn over him, calling him affectionate names, and kiss and hug him. The child soon came to realize his own anger frightened his mother. What initially made the mother anxious now began to affect the child in the same way. In this case the mother did not actually punish anger physically; nevertheless she did "punish" it in her own way. The boy became a neurotic copy of his mother.

This is the typical sequence. At first only the direct expression of anger is punished. But what is once feared only in expression soon comes to be feared even as a feeling. In the past his angry feelings were followed by angry acts—and the acts of anger were punished. He soon learns to be tense when he merely feels angry.

Now the child is at a point where he is afraid not only to express anger but even to feel angry. What then is to happen when something makes him feel genuinely angry? Anger is the natural reaction to frustration. However, in people who have no serious emotional conflicts, these angry feelings rapidly "fade out." In neurotic people, on the other hand, the anger is sustained by a whole host of conflicted and irrational beliefs. The underachiever is neurotic in the sense that he is oversensitive to feelings of anger. And yet his very oversensitivity causes the anger to last. In fact, *were it not for his irrational fears, he would not even interpret many situations as worthy of anger to begin with.* Frustrating incidents occur with high frequency because the underachiever is unconsciously geared to look for trouble. He cannot hold all of it in. Some of the anger must "escape," and indeed it does. One of the ways it can escape is through the development and maintenance of an educational problem.

Very few underachieving children have a clear idea that their poor school grades are caused, even in part, by inner resentment. If you were to ask the typical underachiever if he means to express anger through his poor school work you would almost certainly receive a direct "no" or an expression of confusion for your answer. Most likely he would deny this possibility completely. The underachiever *does* realize his parents are extremely concerned—overconcerned, for that matter—with his achievement. He may even actively dislike their overconcern and constant prodding. He may tell you that his parents constantly nag him. He may feel imposed upon, and annoyed that his parents will not "let up" on him. In spite of his feeling of being imposed upon, he would not realize his poor school work was an indirect expression of resentment and extreme irritation.

The defiance passively expressed through the educational problem is not always due to parental pressure over school work or grades. The anger and irritation have many causes. One of the basic sources of the child's anger is his resentment over a loss of inner freedom. This loss of freedom is often the result of his parents' inability to tolerate the expression of genuine feelings, particularly angry feelings. So the problem perpetuates itself. The typical underachiever is afraid to be himself. He is dissatisfied with himself; he feels inwardly cramped. He feels uncomfortable even when he merely feels angry. He also feels he must live up to unreasonable standards of performance and behavior—another thing that makes him angry. And keep in mind: this anger cannot be expressed through regular channels.

The underachiever is afraid to be spontaneous. He was afraid to express his true feelings when he was young, and may have the same fears throughout life. He learned it was not safe to express any of his true feelings. He may have been taught it is only "safe" to express affection and niceties. This is why many underachievers are so pleasant to be with. Some are uncomfortable expressing anything but affection. The curious thing is that the underachiever, after a while, is also afraid to express genuine affection. His inner annoyance with his parents is so intense that he finds it hard to feel affectionately disposed toward them. Also the inner anger produces such intense feelings of guilt that he is afraid to actually love someone else, and he feels so inwardly guilty he cannot believe anyone could care for him. The guilt feelings make him feel unworthy of love. Furthermore, his poor school work spirals and makes him feel even more unworthy and even more undeserving of love. The vicious cycle aspect of underachievement is met at every turn.

Some parents of underachievers may think that what we have said about the expression of anger is not true in their families. They may feel their underachieving offspring expresses anger and resentment very well—in fact, too well. But three points are important: (1) It is unlikely this child was allowed to feel *free* to express anger, and consequently does not have the sense of inner freedom that should be a part of his personality; (2) even though the child may express anger directly, he probably was and is severely punished for this; (3) the child *is* probably angry a great deal more of the time than he should be. Even though many an underachiever expresses anger openly, it is at great personal expense. And even more important: if he were not so overly sensitive to anger, he would be angry less often.

We do not believe children should go around shouting and expressing their discontents to the world. Children must learn social standards. They themselves would be uncomfortable were they always drawing out the wrath of others by constant temper tantrums. We *do* believe the child should have the feeling he can be angry if he wants to, with no serious or long-lasting ill will from his parents. The ideal is to bring the child up so he is comfortable with the feeling of anger, but knows realistically he is better off not expressing it directly.

The Passive-Aggressive Child Who Is Often Openly Aggressive

People who do not have cramping inhibitions about expressing anger openly actually express anger less often than others. This is especially true in our society. In some societies the open expression of anger is not frowned upon. However, when the members of these societies "blow off steam" they are not expressing genuine anger, but are merely enacting a socially sanctioned "ritual." People who are inhibited or fearful of angry feelings are often loudest in its expression when they do "blow." Many underachievers are inclined to yell their resentments. This is the point that differentiates the forever passive, passive-aggressive child from the passive-aggressive child who does have angry and loud flare-ups. The latter child attempts to get rid of a feared feeling by acting it out. Here is the point: many a child fears the *constant* feeling of anger more than he fears the consequences of one explosive outburst. He tries to trade one explosion for the endless discomfort that accompanies his existence. People very often believe that acting out a feeling will rid them of the feeling. They are doing the very thing they fear, simply because they desperately want to get rid of the feared feeling. Acting angrily on one occasion does not dismiss the *fear* of anger from the nervous system, where it is firmly encoded. And acting angrily on one occasion does not make future anger less likely. Had these children not learned to fear the feeling of anger in the first place, they would not be caught in this impossible situation. (This same thing is true of some types of delinquents.) The feeling of anger so panics these children they do anything to rid themselves of the feeling. They do the very thing they are afraid of. They (wrongly) hope to accomplish two things by these angry outbursts: they desire to bring on punishment from their parents and thereby rid themselves of the guilty feelings which come with the anger; they further desire to get rid of the feelings of anger. Many children try to rid themselves of guilty feelings by taunting and goading their parents into punishing them. Parents can often tell when their children do this. The child believes that if he is punished and "takes his medicine," the unwanted feelings will go away. Neither hope comes true. No one can flee from an inner fear. The children further learn that the tendency can not be spanked away.

The Openly Aggressive Child

One difference between the passive-aggressive child who sometimes expresses anger and defiance openly and the passive-aggressive child who does not is that among the parent couples of the former group there is usually one mate who is loud and arrogant in expressing anger. Strangely enough, it is often that very parent who becomes most angry when the child shows anger. This parent is telling his child he is doomed if he expresses anger, and simultaneously he is providing the child with an aggressive and arrogant model to imitate.

One must understand that the passive-aggressive child is basically terrified by the feeling of anger. If he acts out his anger, it is in a futile attempt to make the feeling go away. One must understand this point in order to see why passive-aggressive children (e.g., underachievers) cannot be "cured" simply by letting them (or ordering them) to behave angrily. Some psychotherapists believe they can cure their inhibited patients by suggesting they openly express their discontents. They end up with inhibited patients who are additionally obnoxious.

A Typical Case

Tommy was in the third grade, doing average work in some subjects, but in danger of failing reading as well as some other subjects. His father was a successful businessman who put much emphasis on competitive success. He spent a good bit of time with Tommy, but constantly overplayed the idea of winning. He sabotaged Tommy in a more subtle way as well. He would not tolerate anger, and became enraged whenever the boy had the "audacity" to be angry. Yet this father himself was loud in his expression of resentments. He often ranted and raved about the house, cursing away, making a noisy disturbance of himself. He was genuinely surprised when Tommy began to do consistently poor work in school. This was Tommy's passive-aggressive retaliation.

Tommy's father taught him two things. He taught Tommy to fear his own feelings of anger. Everytime Tommy showed his anger his father became enraged, and was loud and noisy in his own expression of anger. Tommy "learned" this also. (Psychoanalysts would call this "identification with the aggressor.") Thus Tommy learned two opposite attitudes: He learned that at one and the same time a person should express anger loudly when he feels so inclined, and yet he should fear that anger. This put him in an impossible situation. Tommy became one of those boys who fears anger but expresses it openly. He had a passive-aggressive personality but at the same time had angry outbursts. His fear of anger was actually the more basic feeling. Whenever he could, he used passive, or sneaky, means of expressing defiance. Tommy's father was the type who also demanded that Tommy be a "perfect accomplisher"—a constant victor. Enough critical conditions were met. Tommy became an underachiever.

All passive-aggressive underachievers are similar in that they are using poor school work as a "passive" means of hurting their parents. They have all hit upon underachievement as one means of getting back at their parents and simultaneously punishing themselves for the guilt which attends their basically aggressive orientations.

To round out our understanding of the passive-aggressive person, we might mention a few other types.

Not Only the Underachiever Is a Passive-Aggressive Person

For one, there is the person who is forever saying embarrassing things. At a party he lets you know his job is better than yours. Perhaps he "innocently" remarks that the years have not been too kind to you. He may tell the girls their clothes are not in style, or their cooking not to his taste. This cloddish character is unaware of the fact he is offending practically everyone in sight. He certainly does not realize his true but unconscious intentions are precisely that—to be offensive. He is expressing resentment in a passive-aggressive way. When his behavior is called to his attention he may be genuinely concerned. He may even blush with embarrassment. However, unless some major personality reorientation takes place, it is unlikely his behavior will stay changed for any length of time.

And then there is the person who is always late. No matter the occasion, and no matter how much time he has had to get himself ready, he is late. This "latecomer" is announcing his resentments to the world. He is announcing his irritability over the fact he is not as important as he feels he should be. If this person had more self-assurance, he would not be late so often. One who is consistently late is a passive-aggressive person who feels his lack of security would vanish if only he were more important. He tries to fool himself and the world into thinking he is important by always being late.

The so-called slow child, the "dawdler," who is actually bright but who never acts swiftly or efficiently, is a passive-aggressive individual. He inconveniences others by his slow and inefficient behavior. These children are typically inefficient in their own homes only, or when doing things requested by parents and sometimes by siblings. Very often these "slow children" are not slow in school or when they are visiting a neighbor's house. Among neighbors and employers they can be very conscientious. But at their own homes they are "slow" and exasperating. These slow children are passive-aggressive. They are expressing resentment, but in a devious manner. Usually the parents think this behavior is "cute" when it first occurs, and so do not encourage the child to be more efficient. When the pattern becomes firmly established it is difficult to break. On the other hand, some parents crack down violently on this "slow" behavior at the outset. This does not work either. It increases the inner resentment and convinces the child even more that he should not express anger. So the passive aggressive motive becomes even more compelling. The child becomes even "slower." The more the punishment, the greater the slowness.

There are some individuals—basically bright—who forever seem to be making mistakes that are annoying or expensive, or both, to those with whom they work. They make mistakes that slow down others' work or else are expensive to correct.

As we have seen, underachieving children have passive-aggressive personalities. The Rorschach data mentioned earlier confirm this point. A recent book by one of the authors with Dr. Zygmunt A. Piotrowski and Dr. Edwin Wagner offered some striking confirmation of this same point. The book, *The Hand Test* (Charles Thomas, 1962), was concerned with the prediction of overt aggressive behavior. Among the groups studied was one composed of children with reading problems. These children earned significantly lower acting-out scores than a group composed of "normal" children. These results showed clearly that underachieving children are blocked in their attempts to express resentments openly.

5.

The Sense of Self Worth, the Fear of Failure, and the Ability to Achieve

Every person has some notion of what he or she is "worth." A person with a "healthy" sense of self worth likes himself. He feels he is a reasonably "good fellow." He has good self-confidence, and is appropriately free from guilt feelings. The adult with a healthy sense of self worth thinks of himself as serving some fairly useful social purpose and as being a good husband, father, son, etc. The child with a healthy sense of self worth thinks of himself as being a reasonably nice person who gets along "okay" with his parents, and passably with brothers and sisters. He also feels he is doing reasonably good work in school—work that is about in line with the goals he has set himself. He has fairly realistic expectations about himself and what he can do.

The child with an unhealthy sense of self worth thinks of himself as being a bad and unpleasing child. He feels inwardly that he is disliked by his parents and believes he deserves to be disliked. Naturally he lacks confidence and inwardly distrusts his abilities.

The young child's sense of self worth depends mainly upon the attitudes his parents have toward him. If the parents genuinely love, respect, and admire the child, and convey these attitudes to him, not necessarily in formal speeches, the child will have a healthy sense of self worth.

If the parents are largely displeased with the child, or have unreasonable expectations for him, they will convey these attitudes to the child. The child will think of himself as displeasing and will make unreasonable demands of himself. If the parents place overly intense values on accomplishment, the child will also. Should this happen, the child will imagine he is only as valuable or as "good" as his accomplishment. This is often the case in the families of underachievers.

The parents of the underachiever have made him feel they are interested in him only to the extent that he can achieve or "do things." He feels that aside from potential pride in his accomplishment, they are almost disinterested in him. The parents would not, of course, admit these feelings verbally, but an objective outsider could note that they speak to the child only when they have something to say about school or school grades. Communication is limited to school and school marks.

Ronald's father was a busy man. He realized his business demanded much of his time and felt he could not afford to spend too much time with his child. He did not realize that the *amount of time spent with a child is secondary to the quality of that time.* At any rate, he did realize the importance of a good education. He realized how he himself had lacked an adequate education. He developed a perfectionistic, missionary zeal to make sure Ronald would get an education—a "perfect" one. Ronald was only in the second grade, but as his father saw it, "college will not take him unless his grades are perfect." So Ronald's father spent time with him. He spent just enough time to nag and yell at every bit of Ronald's work that was less than perfect. Ronald absorbed a great deal from his father in the short time they spent together. He absorbed the conviction that nothing less than perfection is tolerable. He absorbed the conviction that his father cared for him only to the extent he could accomplish "perfection." Ronald absorbed the roots of a serious problem of underachievement. He learned to feel his sense of worth depended completely on his accomplishments.

Remember, what we are talking about is a matter of degree. It is certainly desirable for parents to show interest in achievement. There is substantial evidence that a great deal of emphasis is placed upon accomplishment in the families of the best achievers. However, emphasis placed on achievement brings optimal results only if the child has acquired a good degree of confidence in his intellect. If emphasis is placed upon achievement prior to the development of this confidence, it produces negative results.

The Parents of Achievers and the Parents of Underachievers

It is not desirable for achievement to be the sole topic of conversation, or for achievement to be the only communicative "link" between a child and his parents. In the families of underachievers this is too often the case. In the families of the best achievers, emphasis is indeed placed upon accomplishment—but positive attributes are stressed, not negative ones. In the families of achievers, emphasis is placed upon accomplishment by "example," not by "order"; and attention is focused on acting intelligently rather than on accomplishment per se. In fact, there is a great deal of emphasis placed on intelligence by the families of achievers, but little direct pressure is put on the child to "produce." Intelligence and efficiency are stressed as having high values. The parents of underachievers, on the other hand, are usually concerned with achievement and competitive success. Quite often one or both of the parents may show this in his or her own life. The typical parent of an underachiever feels his own status depends on his child's accomplishments.

The underachiever has been made to feel he is only as good as his accomplishments. Thus he feels inept as a person unless his performance standards are at a certain (unreasonable and unrealistic) level. His parents, because of their own tensions, have made him feel he will be unloved unless he always does good work. When the potential underachiever fails something, not only does he feel the grief of a particular and isolated failure, but he feels a complete loss of self worth, and with this his self-confidence. Only when this is realized can one understand why the underachiever so desperately fears to undertake new tasks. When he tries something, his entire sense of confidence is "on the block." A healthy individual will feel the pain of a particular and single instance when he fails something. The potential underachiever experiences a complete loss of confidence and security when he fails the same thing. This explains why minor setbacks have such a devastating effect on the underachiever. It also explains in part why he so desperately fears failure. Any single failure at "one blow" ruins his entire sense of well-being and confidence. Such shaky self-confidence helps to make future failure a greater possibility.

The Growth of Confidence

It is no exaggeration to say that a young *child's* sense of self worth depends almost entirely on what his parents think of him. A child adopts the same attitudes toward himself as his parents have adopted. If the parents love and admire the child, and are fair in their dealings with him, the child will think well of himself. Many parents take this assertion to mean they must never cross the child, that they should not discipline him. A child must be disciplined to teach him the best ways to accomplish his own goals and aims of life. In his early years, the child would soon fall into grave physical danger if he were not disciplined. But if parents are fair, discipline need not be a problem.

As the child grows older, other things begin to have an effect on his sense of self worth, and thereby his self-confidence. The sense of self worth is no longer *directly* related in all instances to the feelings of the parents, although for the majority of people, rationally or irrationally, parental feelings remain the most important ingredients in their sense of self worth. Many adults clearly reveal that when they do something "good," they are usually most anxious to demonstrate this to their parents (or parent substitutes). And from this same source of approval they are anxious to hide their mistakes.

However, other persons and situations in the child's world begin to play a part in the sense of self worth as he grows older. Among these are the attitudes of playmates, the attitudes and feelings of relatives and teachers, and with this the grades and evaluations he receives in school. Later in life, attitudes of co-workers and bosses play a large role. With many people the amount of money earned, the type of job held, social standing in the community, the amount and quality of material possessions, and so forth play an important role in the sense of self worth. None of these things, however, is as important as are the parents' initial attitudes.

It is inevitable that the school's evaluations of the child should have an important bearing on how he feels about himself. It is only natural that good school work should produce good and happy feelings, satisfaction of normal pride, and enhancement of the sense of self worth. And it is only natural that parents should take *some* pride in their child's achievement. We do not mean to imply here that a person should lower his ambition to be more comfortable. We do mean the child should feel "free to fail" without worrying that his entire sense of self worth will be destroyed in the process. When this is the case, he will fail fewer times. When the desire to accomplish becomes all-important in a personality that has the other negative traits we speak of, the actual ability to accomplish decreases. The child no longer feels "free" to make errors, and his tension increases. It is strange but true that the child who does not feel he must accomplish *at all costs* actually accomplishes more than the child who feels desperately compelled to succeed. The active pursuit of perfectionistic excellence, if this be a person's true goal, must come *after*, not before, the development of self-confidence in academic work.

At this point many parents may be saying to themselves: "My child is an underachiever and yet I have never stressed school grades. I never made my child feel he had to get good grades in school." Indeed, it may be true that a big fuss was never made over school grades per se. In many cases of underachievement the parents truthfully report that mention has rarely been made of grades. And this brings us to the crux of the matter. The underachiever does not feel school grades per se are too important; he feels rather that *accomplishment* and *successful* competitiveness are what really count. Something in the home, either in the form of words or deeds, has made the child feel he must always and forever be a "perfect accomplisher."

Keep in mind this is a matter of degree—not an "all or none" proposition. A parent should take some reasonable pride in his child's work. Neither do we mean that the sense of self worth can ever be completely severed from the ability to achieve, especially in Western civilization. Anyone, especially the adult, derives part of his sense of self worth from his ability to do things well. The man who does a good job is proud of this; it enhances his conception of himself. The man who realizes he is doing a poor job usually feels "worthless"—his image of himself is poor. It is only natural that part of the sense of self worth should depend upon accomplishing ability. However, this holds only to a point. The underachieving child believes his *entire* sense of self worth is reflected in his achieving ability, and subsequently in his school grades. This is a psychological distortion —a needless one. Even the man who does a relatively poor job at his place of employment may take pride in being a good husband, father, gardener, etc. The underachieving child has been made to feel everything, but *everything*, depends on his achieving ability.

We have seen some families in which one of the children has equated his entire sense of self worth with his ability to achieve (and developed school problems) for which the parents were not primarily responsible. In these instances a very achievement-oriented and successful older sibling is usually found in the family. Or else it is a family in which the father is very famous or successful. The child on his own just comes to assume the same degree of success and fame is expected of him. In many of these families there is a great deal of implicit emphasis on family name and "standing in the community." The child makes unrealistic assumptions about what is expected of him. He feels his parents secretly expect him to be perfect. In these cases, the parents are not primarily responsible for the achievement-centered orientation around the home. However, these cases are rare. In the majority of underachieving cases where there is a successful older sibling or a famous parent, the finding is also that the parents are irrationally oriented.

An Important Note on High Ambition and Good School Work

We agree with parents that it is desirable for their children to get good grades. We differ with some of them as to what conditions provide the best psychological environment to foster good grades. Even though much of what we have said may sound like a "hands-off" program, its true purpose is to raise the child's self-confidence to a point where he can be a successful competitor. We seek, however, to change the "defining conditions" under which the child works, so that he is free to compete and excel, not compelled to compete. Our purpose is to set forth the psychological conditions which will allow the underachiever to relax to a point where he can accomplish more.

The Active Pursuit of Excellence

Some recent studies have suggested that a successful scientist is motivated by a strong competitive desire to be better and more productive than others. If this is the case, why do we seem to advocate the lessening of the competitive drive? For one thing, the eventual aim is not to lessen the competitive spirit. The aim is to develop sufficient self-confidence in the child so he may translate his wishes for success into actual success. Before a child can really be *successful* at competing, he must have reasonable self-confidence. He must not feel so afraid of failure that he will not tackle jobs to begin with. Successful scientists learned early in their lives to depend on their intelligence and achieving ability. They learned early in life that they could "trust" their "brains." These scientists may have felt, or still feel, uncomfortable with people, but they are not uncomfortable with thinking and with intellectual accomplishment. The underachiever has not learned to depend on his brain. This is a crucial difference. The underachiever lacks self-confidence when it comes to depending upon the results of his thinking. These points show that a strong competitive spirit in the school area may fit in well with some personalities (such as the scientists who participated in these studies) but not with other personalities (such as underachievers). Many a successful scientist early in life lost his self-confidence in dealing with people; however, he did not lose it in connection with the fruits of his thinking. For many scientists there was a tendency to turn more and more to their "brains" precisely *because* their dealings with people were uncomfortable. This does not mean a child has to be uncomfortable with people in order to be smart. The important implication of all these findings is that self-confidence in thinking power must come before or along with the development of a competitively oriented life. When the underachiever has learned to be confident about his thinking ability, he can then "afford" competitiveness. A strong competitive spirit is useless without an adequate degree of self-confidence. The underachiever must first regain confidence in his intellect. Then it does not greatly matter if he becomes overconcerned with ambition and achievement. When the once underachieving child regains self-confidence, he can afford a highly competitive spirit. It is interesting to realize that for an underachiever to eventually value success, he must first be made to devalue competition. In a sense he must devalue it in order to elevate it later.

Avoiding Failure and Pursuing Success: Two Different Things

A retreat from failure is psychologically worlds apart from an active pursuit of excellence. To obtain success, a person must actively pursue goals and take the chance of failing. The individual who is consumed with avoiding failure is afraid to stick his neck out. (Psychoanalysts would consider this an appropriate figure of speech.) The pursuit of excellence is an expansive process—an active process. The avoidance of failure is a restrictive and passive process. The person who wants to avoid failure never risks anything. The pursuit of excellence calls for a concentrated program and involves personal effort. The person who strives for success makes his mind up that he is going to try to succeed. The person who wants to avoid failure makes no commitment. He fears that if he does, there is room for failure. If nothing is attempted, nothing can be failed. He does not make up his mind about anything. One cannot be blamed for failing to obtain something one does not want. The person who fears failure deceives himself into believing he really does not want much from life. First, the underachiever tries to kid himself into believing he is really very intelligent inwardly. Even though he really is, he does not completely believe this. He tries to convince himself he is smart in order to "keep peace" with his parental demand that he be a good and perfect accomplisher. He clings to this belief with astonishing rigidity. He works under such needless pressure that his work is actually poor. Then he tries to kid himself into believing he really does not care about doing good work.

A Magic Solution

The underachiever will not study very much because studying is a commitment. If he studies and still fails, he will have *demonstrated* his failure. The underachiever also feels that a "no exceptions" rule applies to him: he must be the best as far as successful competition is concerned. Here is the paradox. Because he so desperately wants to cling to the inward belief that he is really the "best," he forms a very rigid secret belief. This secret belief is that he is really smart and is really the "best." He thereby *meets the demands for excellence presented by his parents in his imagination if not in reality*. Without realizing it, his parents demand that he be a highly successful accomplisher—or else they will not love him. He "imagines" he is the best. Now they will have to love him—support him—and cherish him. In his own fantasy, he is the perfect person they want. Keep in mind that the underachiever of whom we speak is really bright. But now some strange things happen. For one, he really is not sure of the truth of this "secret" belief, and here is the root of the trouble. The underachiever is really not sure he is as smart and wonderful as he has to pretend to himself. Because he has to feel so utterly perfect, he really doubts himself. No one child could be as perfect as he tries to pretend he really is. Now we come to the core of the problem. *He is afraid to put this belief to the test.* He will not study because studying is a test he might fail in his own eyes. And if that happens, his magic solution would be challenged. And he needs his magic solution. The need to think himself perfect is so irrational that he has to cling to it with all of his psychological tentacles. Only because it is irrational, it creates far more problems than it solves. The whole process makes his school work worse, not better. If he does not study, the prospect of being a failure in his own eyes does not come up. If he has not studied, he cannot really be a failure, for he lets himself off the hook with "I could have done well if I were more interested and studied more." The underachiever is not doing well in school, but at least he has his magic belief that he is really "smart" and "perfect." Should anything happen to his secret belief he would feel totally crushed as a person. He would rather hang on to his "solution by fantasy" than take a chance in the real world. He would rather *imagine* himself perfect than try to prove this in real life by "daring" to study for an examination. For it is possible to fail a real examination. But as long as he commits himself to no definite action his magic belief is invulnerable. As long as he never tries anything, no one can *prove* he is not perfect, and he can keep his magic solution. The secret belief that he is supersmart serves a lot of needs for him. It restores a bit of his self-confidence and makes him feel his parents really love him. He trembles lest anything happen to this image. Part of his personality realizes that his "perfection" image is phony. In the deep recesses of his mind there is an awareness that he clings to a false solution. No wonder he cannot stand challenges. Since he realizes his image of inward perfection is phony, he fears anything which may be a crucial test. The perfection image did not form as a result of doing good work but rather as an imaginary creation to meet an irrational psychological crisis. *The underachiever is compelled to cling to something he knows is unreal.* No wonder he refuses to study, to take his work seriously. He must "look away" from anything that would destroy his imaginary image.

The Secret Thoughts of an Underachiever before a Test

The sequence of thoughts before a test, if it could be verbalized by the underachiever, would run like this. "A test is coming up soon. I really could do very well at it, since I'm really very bright. I had better study for it. But what if I do not do well even after I study—I can't make any excuses for myself then. If I don't study I can always tell myself, no matter what grade I get, that I could have done better had I studied. If I study and still do poorly I won't have any excuses. If I study and still fail, I'll be a *real* failure. It would prove that even when I want to, I can't do a good job. I couldn't stand this. I would rather feel safe and cling to the idea that I could do well if I really wanted to. Even though my work is poor, I still feel safer clinging to the belief that I could do better if I wanted to. This way at least I am not a failure in my own eyes, and I don't even *risk* being a failure in my own eyes. If I don't really try, nobody can say I am a failure."

To be sure, the underachiever may not think these precise words. He may have only the vaguest idea that he is saying these things to himself. One of the most important parts of the psychotherapist's work is to show him that he is really thinking these thoughts. He must be made to see what he actually fears. When the underachiever is made to understand these things, he is on his way to doing better work. However, it is not always easy to do this. The underachiever "looks away" from his real problems and fears. He tries to pretend these processes are not actually going on. It is often difficult to get him to take a clear view of himself.

How Does the Underachiever "Excuse" Himself?

At a conscious level the underachiever often tries to convince himself that his poor school grades reflect a lack of interest. At a conscious level, underachievers invent all kinds of excuses for their poor work. They hardly ever realize they are desperately afraid to fail—so afraid that they will not commit themselves to a program of study.

Only when the underachiever realizes that his entire security is not at stake in everything he does will he do better work. Only when he feels "free" to fail will he actually fail fewer times. A central message of this book is that people who feel "free" to fail —that is, a single failure would not be a mortal blow to total security—fail less frequently than people who passionately fear failure.

6.

The Fear of Being Ordinary, and
Pride in Failure: A Paradox

The tremendous emphasis placed upon accomplishment coupled with the fear of failure can produce some rather striking side effects. One of these side effects is a fear of being ordinary. Another possible side effect is the development of a deep-seated conviction one must constantly work "hard" in order to be loved. When a child begins to feel he must *always* work hard, he will often "throw in the towel," feeling that if this is what life is all about, it simply is not worth it.

Naturally we are not speaking against excellence or accomplishment. These things are valued and rewarded by our society. The crucial differences between achievers and nonachievers are often differences in degree, not always of kind. Almost any normal individual in our society feels he must be productive to be worthy of love, support, and admiration. Probably few normals in our society think themselves "merely ordinary." But a desire to be excellent is wasted on an individual who lacks self-confidence, especially self-confidence having to do with the uses of intelligence. A strong desire to accomplish is wasted on a person who cannot transform his wishes into purposeful and directed activity.

One Relationship between Self-Confidence and Good Work

One relationship between self-confidence and good work is circular. Self-confidence should be reasonably strong before a person places a high premium on excellence and accomplishment. At the same time, self-confidence is in large part derived from the ability to do work *which is acceptable to or in keeping with the self picture.* If a person starts out by assuming that the impossible is expected of him, he will not develop self-confidence. Obviously, then, in order to develop good self-confidence an individual should not expect the impossible from himself when he is in his young and formative years. Self-confidence must "take root" and grow in order for excellent accomplishment to be eventually possible. Self-confidence cannot grow if the person starts right out by assuming perfection is expected of him. And this is what he will expect if this is what his parents expect.

Seen in this light, the fear of being ordinary, which plagues many underachievers, is another reflection of their fear of failure and of the deep-set belief they will lose the love of their parents if they are not "perfect." The fear of being ordinary has some interesting side effects of its own.

The fear of being ordinary *sustains* underachievement in a very peculiar way.

Some underachievers so fear to be ordinary that they come to "like" the fact they do poor work in school. At least then they are not ordinary.

The trouble starts when the child equates the idea of being an excellent accomplisher with the idea of being non-ordinary. He feels extraordinary things are expected. The very intensity of this expectation rules out the possibility of his being a standout. But the desire to be extraordinary remains. When this happens, the child begins to take some secret pleasure in the fact that he is doing poor work. For now he is a standout—albeit a negative standout.

This state of affairs is summed up in the diagram. The figure

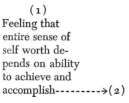

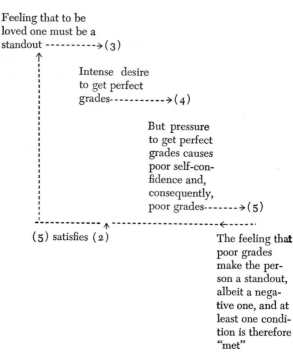

(1)
Feeling that entire sense of self worth depends on ability to achieve and accomplish--------→(2)

Feeling that to be loved one must be a standout ----------→(3)

Intense desire to get perfect grades-----------→(4)

But pressure to get perfect grades causes poor self-confidence and, consequently, poor grades-------→(5)

(5) satisfies (2)

The feeling that poor grades make the person a standout, albeit a negative one, and at least one condition is therefore "met"

shows that the underachiever starts out with fear of failure caused in large part by an irrational belief, namely, that his entire sense of self worth depends on his ability to achieve and accomplish perfectly. From this, he comes to feel he must be a standout. Naturally his first inclination is to be a standout by virtue of perfect grades. The very intensity of the need for perfect grades works against its own fulfillment. He is too tense and conflicted to get excellent grades. Then how about being a standout by virtue of poor grades? That part of his personality which strongly desires to be a standout will at least be satisfied. Getting poor grades at least makes him dissimilar from the majority of his friends.

Freud clearly demonstrated that opposite tendencies and wishes can exist side by side in the human nervous system. Each wish and motive may carry on a life of its own, seemingly oblivious to the presence of other desires at odds with it.

Even though failure and poor work scare a certain part of the personality of the underachiever, another part is happy with the idea of poor grades, for these at least set one apart. Like a person who craved sweets and limited his diet to saccharine and water, at least part of the personality of the underachiever is gratified by the "distinction" of having poor grades.

The underachiever who comes to secretly glorify his underachievement must have these facts pointed out to him. This is no easy matter. First of all, these mental processes are rarely formed into logical, verbal units in the mind of the underachiever (although their derivatives may be). Secondly, many underachievers do not realize they take secret pride in their poor work. Many do, however, brag about how little school means to them. They are "rugged individualists."

The underachiever does not glory in poor marks per se. He tries, rather, to glorify his approach to life in general and to not studying in particular. Why should he conform? Why should he study? That is for the masses, the sheep. However, it is one thing for a true individualist with basic self-confidence to utter these thoughts to himself and quite another for the fearful and insecure underachiever to have the same thoughts. In the first instance, true individualism springs at least in part from honest beliefs, rooted in adequate self-confidence. In the second instance, the "individualism" is as phony as a three-dollar bill. It springs from a defensive fear of commitment. If one is too frightened to pursue something, what better excuse is there than to assert the thing is not wanted. And to boot, this maneuver makes a liability sound like an asset. How easy: poor school grades reflect "individualism." Not only does the underachiever hope to salvage his wounded pride with this deceit, but he makes himself a rugged hero as well. His poor studying habits are not due to fear and insecurity but to rugged individualism.

Many underachievers develop the deep-seated conviction that one must work hard in order to survive. This is true of many people in our culture. There is ample evidence all around us of the ways in which our society rewards aggressive competitiveness and no-holds-barred ambitiousness.

The equation between the entire sense of self worth and the ability to achieve also contributes to the overdevelopment of this conviction. The child comes to believe psychological security comes only to those who work hard all the time. The child comes to believe relaxation is bad. This may sound strange, for the underachiever certainly does not always seem to act in keeping with this fear. The cloak of laziness the underachiever so easily wears conceals many hidden guilts, one of them having to do with relaxation. The "laziness" is but a cover for the fact he feels life is so hard and so much perfection is required that one might as well not start. But just because he says this to himself does not mean he believes it.

7.

The Fear of
Success

One of the most surprising things demonstrated by Freud was that people not only may fear failure, but may fear success as well. This kind of person cannot win. History furnishes many examples of people who psychologically could not tolerate success. We often read of people who take their own lives while at the crest of personal success and popularity. A good number of these people were psychologically petrified by the idea that they were "succeeding." Success-fearing individuals do not always long to fail. In fact they are disappointed or even afraid of failure. But they are even more afraid of success.

Why Do Certain People Fear Success?

What strange thing actually makes a person go to great pains to avoid success?

Examples of this are varied. A very famous opera star of this century abruptly retired from an active career at the height of her vocal power and in spite of incredible popularity. Another famous movie star of a few years ago retired from public life under much the same conditions. Many well-known businessmen have committed suicide just after having experienced marked successes. On a more ordinary level, there are certain individuals who experience a depressive letdown accompanied by tension after completing something that usually would cause victory celebrations.

We are not prepared to explain all of these kinds of reactions here, for there is certainly no single explanation that can account for them.

The scientist or author who works a long, long time in completing a project or book often experiences a letdown when the task is completed. However, this may not mean he fears success. His experience is akin to mourning—much like the grief one experiences at losing someone who has been a close and constant companion. A very similar thing occurs when a person experiences "grief" after completing a project that he had yearned to do since childhood.* The completion of this task leaves the person with the feeling of "Where do I go from here?" He may feel there is little meaning left in life. He has fulfilled his "life goal." He feels purposeless and dejected. Typically, however, he soon finds something else that becomes a "life goal." The majority of these individuals spring back, to take on new creative tasks.

The fear of success is termed by psychoanalysts a fear of Oedipal victory. An approximate explanation is that a person fears success because he mentally equates success with surpassing or "outdoing" a loved but feared parent. This fear is much more characteristic of men than of women. Men who suffer from this fear live in dread that they will surpass or be victorious "over" their fathers. Unconsciously they fear that such a "victory" will call forth aggressive vengeance from the father, or will alienate

---

* Psychoanalysts might interpret this in terms of forbidden Oedipal fulfillment. This explanation would be incomplete, however, in the majority of instances.

an irrationally overvalued source of support. The man or child who has this fear imagines unconsciously his father will not stand for any competition from him, and imagines the father will not allow any "victory" to go unpunished. The analysts believe the "original" competitive situation is that between the father and son competing for the exclusive possession of mother. The child comes to feel that any personal "victory" is psychologically the same thing as "robbing" mother from father. The analysts consider that the child (or grown man) reacts to this possibility as though the father would then actually harm him (the son) physically.

Whether or not one accepts all of these ideas, one should recognize that rivalry does exist beween fathers and sons. Many fathers, usually unconsciously, harbor secret resentments against their male children, particularly the first born. The father had come to look upon his wife as his exclusive property. He has doubts about whether her being a mother will change his own position with her. He is actually a bit jealous of the little, new-born arrival. Many fathers harbor this jealousy a long time. The father's relationship with his own parents has much to do with how he reacts to sharing his wife's affection with the new arrival. Because of insecurity, many a father is oversensitive to the amount of attention given the child, and he begins to feel insecure about his own place in his wife's eyes. In addition, he may have secret resentments against his own father, and then unconsciously suspect his own child has the same feelings toward him. There are many, many reasons for the competitive hostility that often exists in exaggerated degrees between a father and son. When the competitive hostility is too intense, the father will communicate to the son the idea that he (the father) does not want the son as competitor. The father indicates that they can be friends only so long as the son will be submissive and not be a competitor.

If this child wants to retain the friendship of his father, he must make a pact with himself never to excel at anything. Any excellent bit of work reminds him that he may be "sinning" against his father. The child may very well fear actual physical harm from his father. Any evidence that he is being successful will be interpreted by the child as a transgression. The child feels any personal success will do nothing but earn him a powerful enemy.

The Underachiever's Dilemma

If this state of affairs between father and son exists in a family that demands perfection and accomplishment, the child is really in a bind. On the one hand, excellent accomplishment is expected. On the other hand, a passive submission to the father is expected. The problem will remain until the child and his parents can be made to see that two different reactions are being demanded of the child at one and the same time.

Rudolph was a child eight years old in the third grade. Both of his parents were bright—but status crazy. They wanted their child to be at the top of his class academically. Rudolph's father was bright but frustrated. He felt his status in life was not appropriate to his considerable but "hidden" talents. He believed other people lacked the ability to recognize what he had to offer the world. This father was deeply dependent on his wife, who spent a good bit of her time flattering him and siding with him against the world. The more dependent the husband-father became on his wife, the less inclined he became to share her with anybody—whether this "sharer" was his own son or not. Rudolph felt his father resented him from the start. Were Rudolph to approach his mother with even the mildest request, his father, if present, would say: "Rudolph, stop bothering your mother." The father became very angry whenever his wife had to spend time with Rudolph. Whenever Rudolph would say anything, his father would point out his son's lack of "real" understanding. Surprisingly enough, the father did not resent three other children, one a boy, who followed Rudolph. The father had Rudolph as a scapegoat. This father would tolerate Rudolph only if he were submissive and withdrawn. Rudolph learned that the only way to keep his father happy was to flatter him and acquiesce to his demands. At the same time, this father demanded that Rudolph get good grades. Rudolph became an underachiever—but one caught in a double-barreled trap. Not only did his father demand that he never fail anything, but he also demanded, without realizing it, that Rudolph never succeed at anything. At the time of this writing Rudolph and his family are receiving psychotherapy.

A girl may also have a fear of success. The closest parallel situation to the boy's would be one in which the girl psychologically equates doing good work with being competitively better than her mother. She then interprets good work on her part as an aggressive act against her mother. It is likely that the "primary" competitive hostility of the girl child is with the mother for the exclusive love of the father. However, the girl's situation does not really parallel the boy's for many reasons. Chief among these is the fact that competition and aggression play different roles in the lives of wives and mothers than in those of fathers and husbands. Also, the relationship between a mother and any of her children, male or female, is different from those between fathers and children.

A child may have a fear of failure, and this is bad enough. He may fear success, and this is unfortunate. The child who fears both failure and success is really in trouble, for he cannot win no matter what he does.

8.

Aggression and
Competition

Everyone in Western society links aggressiveness and competitiveness to some extent in their minds. An intense desire to do well is usually motivated in part by a desire to aggressively outdo others. Aggressiveness and competitiveness are not independent things: it is hard to find some of one without finding some of the other. A person who is afraid to feel or show anger finds it difficult to maintain a competitive attitude. Aggressiveness does not "cause" competitiveness, but if the capacity for aggressiveness is lacking, there will be little competitiveness. A bit of the fuel, so to speak, for competition comes from aggressive attitudes. In a strict sense, competition implies that at least two people are "fighting" each other for something that only one of them can possess. This is true of school grades when they are distributed on the basis of the so-called normal curve. The normal-curve method of assigning grades limits the number of persons who can be given any particular grade. There are a limited number of high grades, and only a certain number of students can be awarded these grades. So in a very real sense, what one person gets is "taken away" from another person. There is certainly an aggressive element directly present here.

The linkage between aggression and competition is uppermost in the minds of some people. These people carry such feelings over into their entire life process. This type of individual imagines that anything good which happens to him means something "bad" happens to someone else. In very pathological cases this may even carry over to food, water, and air. The very emotionally ill person may imagine that when he is eating or breathing he is "taking" food or air away from someone else.

There is a very real aggressive element present in competitive situations. The term "aggressive" here refers not only to directly aggressive actions, but to the fact that people compete for scarce or limited resources. This means that what one person gains is taken away from someone else.

In order to compete with any efficiency, a person must not be overly frightened by angry attitudes. For if the person is frightened by anger he will be frightened by all aggressiveness to some extent, and hence he will be frightened by competitiveness.

The underachiever very much desires to do better work than others, but he sees this as being "aggressive." And even aggressive *feelings* make him uncomfortable, let alone aggressive *acts*.

9.

Inner Doubts

This trait is not as universal among underachievers as are the others already mentioned. Remember: this trait, like the others, comes in a wide variety of "intensities." For one child the fear of anger may be extra-intense. For another child the fear of failure may be extra-intense. For still another child the linkage between anger, aggression, and competition may be extra strong. Some children may have a very rigid idea of what they must do and accomplish in order to be loved and supported. For other children this expectancy may not be so rigid. It is the presence of a number of these traits, or of a few in tremendous intensities, that produce underachievement.

Many underachieving children are obsessional in orientation. The child with an obsessional orientation rarely has a clear-cut feeling about anything or anyone. Further, he distrusts his own abilities. He will spend a great deal of time worrying about things. There is nothing very adaptive about this kind of brooding. If the underachiever would spend this same time preparing himself and studying, he would be in a far more fortunate position. However, he does not do this. The underachiever will try to convince himself studying is not important, that he is really not interested in it anyhow, and then will spend much time worrying and brooding about how poorly he is doing. What he will not do is realistically prepare his work—the one thing that would actually help him.

Many fathers of underachievers themselves have passive-aggressive streaks. This type of father may have had achievement problems himself when he was young. He may now use his own eventual success as an argument to avoid helping his child. Many a father will say, "I see no reason to do anything about the boy's problem. I was like this myself." These fathers call themselves "late bloomers," forgetting their own children may have more severe problems than they. Underachievement often builds up from generation to generation, usually in increasing intensities.

Many fathers of underachievers punish by sarcasm. They think they are clever, and congratulate themselves because they do not stoop to physical punishments. How wrong they are. There are few things that destroy confidence so well as sarcasm. A subtle, mocking sarcasm directed at a bright child is the surest way to destroy his confidence.

The underachiever both wants to please and displease his parents at the same time. On one level he wants to get good marks to win affection. At the same time, part of his personality balks at the pressure under which he must work. He has the feeling that he must get good grades. This angers him—and he resents the pressure. Consequently, he both wants and does not want to get good grades. He is working at cross-purposes with himself.

10

Low Frustration Level

The Child Who Never Finishes Things

The typical underachiever is easily frustrated. He will not stay with a task for any length of time. He stays with it to the point where things get a little tough. Then he quits. He typically starts many tasks but completes few. This trait is not peculiar to the underachiever. Many excellently achieving children appear to behave similarly. However, in the achieving child the flitting about does not reflect a low frustration level. It reflects wide, albeit restless, interest in many, many things—a strong, natural curiosity which embraces a wide range of phenomena. It may partially reflect these very same things in the underachiever, for he too is curious. But in the underachiever, listlessness and an inability to complete a task are more often related to a low "boiling point." In the underachiever the inability to complete a task reflects an inability to tolerate frustration.

A low level of frustration means that the person's self-confidence and endurance crumble at the first sight of even a minor setback. The child becomes flustered, may even "blow up." The quality of the work goes down, and he may abandon what he is doing altogether. A main cause of low frustration tolerance is a rigid and unrealistic self image that will not tolerate the possibility of failure. Other causes relate to the level of psychosexual maturity attained by the child, and hence have to do with his entire adjustment.

The underachiever cannot tolerate even the possibility of failure. He demands instantaneous success because even the most minor setback reminds him that he might be a total failure. This fear is so intense that his self-confidence abandons him when there is even the slightest possibility of failure. This is why the underachiever will work at something only so long as he is being successful. This is why the underachiever will not get interested in a thing unless he firmly knows he can be good at it.

Underachievers, like many neurotics, want to start out with "instant success." They would like to start at the end. They are afraid to go through intermediate steps—steps not only necessary but often part of the fun for others. The underachiever wants to be an immediate success.

How do these various maneuvers, this flitting about and listlessness, present themselves to the conscious mind of the underachiever? He tries to tell himself he is "not really interested" in any project that gives him trouble. He would rather believe he feels no interest than admit he has a tremendous fear of failure.

He is often irritable whenever he is challenged. He wants to blame others. Most underachievers are poor sports. They may even shift blame when there is no need to do so. The underachiever will often think his friends are going to blame him for something (like a badly played baseball or a fumbled catch) when there are no such intentions. The underachiever will gruffly mumble a loud curse upon his "misplay" and immediately begin to make excuses, blaming just about everything in sight except himself.

When the underachiever is able to develop a more realistic

self picture, when he no longer feels his entire sense of self worth rides on everything attempted, his level of frustration tolerance will improve. He no longer will demand instant success or "nothing." He will not only be able to go through the steps necessary for earning success, but may even enjoy himself in the process.

11

The Tendency to Regress:
The Babyish Child

The technical definition of regression involves differential "fixation" points and structural properties of biological energy systems. For our purposes, the word refers to a tendency to revert back to more infantile patterns of behavior in times of stress. It occurs when the current personality configuration lacks a nonconflicted way of handling the stress. The person who regresses falls back to ways of handling things which may have been effective and even appropriate at a younger age but which may or may not be effective in the current situation. We all have some tendency to regress. For this reason, the term "regressive tendency" is reserved for those people who show a *marked* and *definite* tendency. In practice, the term "regressive" points to infantile, usually noneffective ways of dealing with current situations. Examples of regressive behavior include yelling at inanimate objects for mistakes made by oneself (this is a carryover of the infant's belief that objects are really alive and may behave "meanly"), becoming tearful in mildly stressful interpersonal situations (the tearful person is demanding to be "let off the hook" and so asks for pity rather than annoyance), becoming babylike and "cute" when things are going poorly (this is a desire to demand love and to drop personal responsibility, since a baby cannot be held personally responsible). Regressive behaviors vary in the degree to which they are regressive. For example, a marked degree of regressiveness is shown by that individual who just "closes his eyes" and waits and hopes for difficult issues to improve. This type of denial is in part a carryover of the child's very primitive belief that bad things will go away if he passively waits. This childish belief is frequently carried over into adult life. The adult who uses this maneuver just looks away from things, hoping the conflicted issues will magically improve on their own. Most psychosomatic reactions are regressive. The body reflects or acts out the conflicts which cannot be verbalized.

Regressive behavior is not only caused by differential fixation points and defects in psychological development; the underachiever has other reasons for acting in a regressive manner.

The underachiever actually hopes to gain quite a bit from regressive maneuvers. If the unconscious attitudes of the child could speak up in regular, rational, verbal units, they would say something like the following: "My parents say they will not love me unless I produce and accomplish. But I try and I can't. If they do not love me, then I'm in big trouble. After all, my parents insure that I go on living. They give me water and food and they protect me. It is important that they love me. But they say they will love me only if I do good work, and if I am always the 'best' and most excellent. Why do they place so many conditions on their love? Why do they make these demands? Why do I have to meet obligations in order for them to love me? When I was a baby they loved me, and I wasn't doing anything particularly 'good.' They just loved me because I was a baby. I guess a baby does not have to meet any obligations. Maybe that's the answer. If I were a baby they would love me, and nothing would be required on my part. It would be their duty to love me, and they wouldn't demand anything in return. I wouldn't have to get good grades. I wouldn't have to have any personal responsibility at all." And so it goes. The underachiever reverts to infantile ways of thinking and feeling in an attempt to regain and maintain the love of his parents. He feels they only give their love when he can "come across" with excellent work. But the love given to a baby is unconditional love (in nonpathological parents). If the underachiever becomes a baby, then his parents would have to love him, just as they would a baby. He would not even have to worry about school grades. In fact, he would not have to do anything. And so the underachiever hopes to rid himself of a great many problems in one fell swoop. Much is at stake, but he believes he can gain much. He believes he can regain the love and support of his parents, and with this, his sense of self worth and confidence. Furthermore he can gain all of these things very passively. And so, without even realizing what he is doing on a conscious level, he "becomes" a baby. Increasingly his parents notice he is acting like a baby. He whines now instead of talking. He has temper tantrums, cries, and fights with his younger brothers and sisters more frequently. He demands more time and attention of his parents than before. In short, he becomes a baby in a more fully grown child's body. (A child is most likely to adopt this orientation if he has a younger sibling. He sees the new arrival getting plenty of affection and having to meet no obligations in return.)

Unfortunately these maneuvers do not work. In fact, regressive behavior usually does not accomplish any of its objectives. Mainly, it does not win and maintain parental love. The parents are annoyed by regressive behavior, and it drives them even further from the child. Since regressive behavior is rarely effective, it creates more serious problems than existed at the outset. And so the problems become even more intense, and the more intense the problems become, the more the regressive behavior is called into operation. The more the child thrashes, the tighter his bonds become.

Regressive behavior generally fades out when at least two conditions are met. For one thing, the child must be made aware of the ineffectiveness of his behavior patterns. Secondly, the child must be made to feel secure in the love and support of his parents, while at the same time his irrationally intense "need" for this love must be reduced.

Occasionally, regressive behavior is partially successful for the child. Sometimes one (or both) of the parents, because of some personal problem, is "swayed" by babyish behavior. A parent occasionally thinks his or her little child is "cute" when acting regressively (and usually annoying everyone present except the doting parent). It is unfortunate when this happens. The child who is "excused" from work and responsibility on the basis of regressive behavior soon discovers that he has a powerful and awesome weapon in his hands to control his parents. The weapon will soon be used in other areas. Soon the parents discover to their horror that they are living with a ruthless tyrant. A parent who is swayed by regressive behavior usually has intense personality conflicts. At best, the parent is powerfully mixed up about the involved child. Even though a parent may allow the child to get away with things, the parent's love is not a consistent or non-conflicted love.

In the typical case, the regressive maneuvers adopted by the child in an attempt to take out insurance on the love of the parents fails in its aim. The parents are antagonized, and the situation becomes worse. What the child hoped would be a comprehensive solution to his problems turns out to be a comprehensive nightmare for the entire family.

12.

Poor Performance
in Class

Man is basically a social animal. Normally, his most important decisions take into account the feelings and reactions of other persons. The human child is very sensitive to others, particularly to his parents. The child learns that how others evaluate him is important for his own safety and well-being. A negative evaluation by others can cause hurt, just as a negative evaluation from his parents caused hurt when he was much younger. For most people the evaluations of the parents continue to play a prime role. In fact, most people think of their parents as the important "evaluators" even after they are grown and married, although many might deny this as far as conscious feelings are concerned. The reason why parents, or the attitudes learned from parents, continue to play such important roles in our lives is that these attitudes were engendered in us when we were most impressionable. This is unfortunate in many ways. Realistically speaking, the way parents "evaluate" their adult children is of minor consequence. However, adults tend to *think* and *act as if* parental evaluations were of extreme importance. These adults are unrealistically shackled to the past.

Most significant fears are learned—at least in "bud" form—in childhood. There is little use in denying that the personality is mainly formed throughout the childhood years. These are the years in which the parents are literally "everything" to the child. No wonder one remains sensitive to parents' feelings and reactions.

When the child enters school he transfers some of his parent-directed feelings to his teacher. The teacher becomes the "mother" when the child is away from home. The child now wants good evaluations from the teacher. Good evaluations mean increased support and well-being in general.

The child soon sees his little friends and peers as evaluative sources. What they say and think of him, the extent to which they invite him to join their games, and the extent to which they seek him out and look upon him as a worthy companion, are seen as evaluations.

Actually, however, just about all of the important evaluations which make a child an underachiever take place in the home. For the most part, school only brings out, intensifies (or stifles), what is already in the child in nascent form.

The Improving Child Who Fails to Show Gains in School

Though many underachievers show good educational gains after being tutored, many never show or can use these gains in the actual school classroom. Something about the school situation prevents them from being able to demonstrate the gains which are so obvious in the tutoring sessions.

The child has been tested and tutoring begun. He does very well in the tutoring sessions. His tutor is pleased with the progress. More achievement tests are administered. Sure enough, the child has made significant advances. His school performance is still the same: poor.

The most general reason, of course, is that the child is still too tense in school. He tenses up when called upon to perform, or when asked to recite aloud. He knows his work before the examination, but it "disappears" when the test papers are handed out. In a school recital all his friends are watching him. The teacher is there, to evaluate and criticize him. The tension is much greater than during a tutoring session. In class, people are psychologically "looking over his shoulder," ready to criticize and make fun of him should he do a poor job—or so he believes.

But there is another reason. The educational problem is, in part, the child's defiant anger directed at the parents. It represents his "revenge" for the inhibiting conditions under which they have made him live. The teacher and the school situation itself are equivalent to parental authority in his mind—the authority against which he rebels. The teacher, as the "mother away from home," is reacted to by the child as if she were the actual mother. The conflicts which exist in the child's mind in relation to his parents are played out in school. Also, the child may perceive his peers as siblings, and hence react even more irrationally.

The individual tutor, if he or she is a good one, does not criticize the child, but on the contrary is very accepting and tolerant. Consequently, the defiant reaction usually does not occur in the tutoring session. The most important thing to be "taught" in the tutoring situations is not just specific content materials, like science or reading, but rather *self-confidence*. If the tutoring sessions do not help lift the child's self-confidence (along with his knowledge), they are not doing all they could. Content tutoring alone, in the case of the underachiever, is like putting a patch over an area where reconstruction is required.

Any underachiever who after a suitable length of time (six months), fails to show progress with tutoring alone, would do well to receive psychotherapy along with the tutoring.

13

The Overprotective
Mother

It has become fashionable in psychology to talk about the "overprotective" mother. This is an unfortunate choice of words. The term "overprotective" is used popularly to single out the mother who literally "swarms" over her child, rarely allowing him to do anything for himself. Supposedly the child does not develop inner strength because he becomes used to having things done for him. Further, he fails to develop a clear sense of independent identity. When the child of an overprotective mother develops an educational problem, he is thought to be expressing anger and annoyance toward the mother, who literally will not give him room in which to live, and/or that he is incapable of independent action. All of this is correct, as far as it goes.

However, these so-called overprotective mothers are not just overprotective. Actually, overprotective moods alternate with irritable and rejecting moods. Of course the child is deeply impressed in a negative way by the extreme contrast in moods he sees in his mother. The overprotective mother has an erratic personality. One moment she appears to be loving and full of concern; the next moment she is anxious and irritable.

The overprotective mother is usually frightened by her own feelings of anger toward her child. She overstresses a nervous type of love and affection, doling these out until the child, like an addict, comes to depend upon them as though they were the be-all and end-all of existence. A mother who constantly and anxiously overplays love and affection in her relationship with her child, eventually makes him completely dependent on her. He cannot separate his own attitudes from his mother's. He does not know where she "leaves off" and he "begins." Mixed in with this dependence is anger and annoyance. Our observations show that the anxious affection meted out to these children, is a serious pathology-producing agent. The mother's moods vary a great, great deal, and these extreme contrasts are every bit as damaging as overprotectiveness per se.

It is particularly damaging for a parent to show a hatefully rejecting attitude toward the child. "Experts" say lately that mothers or fathers should feel free to vent anger whenever they feel like it. "Why not?" they say. "The parents are human too." But if this is a chronic state of affairs, they are going to pay a high price for their ventilation. They would do well to consider the difference between realistic discipline and hateful rejection. Parents should not avoid discipline. However, it is one thing to discipline and it is another thing to make the child feel he is hateful and disgusting. Children pay little attention to words. They watch the expression on the face and the tone of the voice. When these "nonverbal communicators" say "I hate you, you lousy pain in the neck, and I'm furious," the child feels hated. There is no point in making a speech to the child, as has recently been the vogue, saying, "I love you but I hate your actions." This makes no sense to the child when he can read your face and tone of voice.

The overprotective mother lacks a feeling of inner freedom; she probably has intense but inhibited anger at her own mother, associated with the feeling that her own child is a test case by means of which she is constantly evaluated. She has a hard time recognizing that her child is a unique and distinct person. She confuses her own goals with the child's, and is unable to relax. She feels that if she does not take personal charge of things, some sort of "catastrophe" is sure to result. She sees her children as extensions of herself, and is too intimately linked with them. She feels other people and her own "internalized" mother evaluate her by means of the child. For these reasons, she swarms over her child, allowing him little personal freedom. But because the burden under which she lives is so intense, because she herself has the feeling she is constantly being evaluated, akin to the feeling of the underachiever, she also harbors a great deal of repressed resentment. This resentment usually expresses itself as irritability. The overprotective mother is notorious for becoming irritated at trifles and for her bossy handling of others. Leadership capacity which flows from self-confidence is very different from a desire to dominate, which is based on insecurity and nervous irritability.

We have shown that the term "overprotective" does not do justice to the phenomena, because the mother is just as often in an irritable mood as in an "overprotective" one, which in addition to being unpleasant, makes her behavior seem extra inconsistent and therefore frightening. If "overprotective" just means the mother does a lot for the child—even too much—it would not be true that overprotectiveness could explain any cases of underachievement. For one thing, mothers of some of the best achievers, often the very best, are overprotective, if we mean by this "doing too much for the child." If the mothers of some of the best achievers are constantly doing too much for their children, then overprotectiveness in this sense of the word cannot easily be used as an explanation for underachievement.

Here is the point: it is not the doing of too much per se which is responsible for an unfavorable reaction in the child. The unfavorable reaction is caused by the doing of too much plus many other things, three in particular. First, there is irritability. Anyone who feels "totally responsible" for everything would naturally be irritable.

Secondly, the child becomes very dependent on his mother. But at the very same time the mother, on the surface, is requesting independent behavior. Unconsciously the mother is forcing the child to be dependent—to feel he can never do things as well as she, and that he might as well never try to "leave" her. At the same time, she consciously would like to take pride in his independent, stand-on-his-own-feet behavior. So she is both inhibiting the development of independent self-confidence in her child by making him dependent on her, and demanding that he be exactly what she will not allow him to be: independently self-confident. The overprotective mother would explain that she just "enjoys" doing things for her child and that this is why she allows him to do so little for himself. Unconsciously she has a need to control him. She is insecure and wants to leave nothing to chance.

The children of overprotective mothers generally become very dependent. But at the same time they deeply resent these dependency needs. They resent them because on another level the mother has demanded that the child show initiative and independence. She fails to see the relation between her swarming all over her child and his lack of self-confidence. The overprotective mother always wants her attitudes adopted, her opinions honored, her ideas considered best, and in general to be "boss." She makes the child feel he cannot hope to compete with her wonderfully "self-confident" efficiency. Although the overprotective mother may be efficient, she is far from genuinely self-confident. Her need to control comes from nagging inner doubts about her own identity. She has a fierce pride and feels she must be "best." One reason she is not an underachiever is that her lack of self-confidence does not extend into the area of intellectual functioning. She trusts her intelligence and knows she can do acceptable (maybe excellent) work. Her lack of self-confidence has to do with a general feeling something "awful" will happen unless she is "alert"—ever vigilant and in command. Her lack of confidence, then, has to do with the burdensome feelings produced by the mere process of having to live and carry out daily routine chores. She is unable to relax, and sees life as a series of challenges which must be met. At a deeper level, her difficulties involve consciously unacceptable angers and resentments, and inability to achieve an independent sense of identity. It is usually necessary, but difficult, to get the overprotective mother involved in a psychotherapeutic process.

The third important thing which seems to go on in such families is very insidious, difficult to spot, but capable of causing a lot of trouble. It is this: displays of affection are given with anxiously excessive frequency and intensity, and then when the child comes to depend on these displays as an addict depends on his drug, the threatened withdrawal of affection is used as a terrible weapon. The threatened loss of affection is reacted to as if it were an earth-shaking, death-bringing event. Now it is true that affection and its withdrawal is used a behavior regulating device in many societies, particularly in ours. Affection and good feeling are particularly valued in this society. But the overprotective mother uses affection like a war club—she metes it out to reward those things which glorify her, and withholds it whenever she feels challenged or thwarted. The child is literally an addict, and the mother the "pusher" (in many senses of the word). The husband or father in such families is typically on the passive and retiring side—if not at the start of the marriage, then soon after.

Our main concern with the child of the overprotective mother is with his self-confidence and achieving ability. His mother has made him feel quite dependent; but at the same time he has been taught dependency feelings are wrong. Unconsciously, and even consciously, she expects him to lean on her, to trust her implicitly, to take her advice without question, and to refer all difficult problems to her. At the very same time, also consciously (but the contradiction does not occur to her), she expects him to stand on his own two feet and to "perform" for her at her beck and call. She expects him to do things that will shower glory on her for the fine job she is doing with his upbringing. At an early age this might take the form of her demanding that the child say hard words for an audience. She likes to "show him off" to the crowd—not to a normal but to an excessive degree. If the child reacts to these demands in a negative way, she immediately will threaten him with lack of affection, either by words or actual deed. She feels as though she has been mortally offended, as if the child has betrayed her. She brags about her child to an untoward degree. She expects him to be aggressive when playing with other children and to "stand up for his rights," even though she has prepared him for nothing of the sort. On the contrary, she has taught him to refer all problems to her. At a later age she expects the child to consider her opinion as the most important in the world. She expects him to continue to do excellent work that will reflect the glories of her personality and upbringing. She may even expect the attention from him that a wife would ordinarily expect from a husband. In all probability, her husband is not too interested in her and tries to avoid her a good bit of the time. She robs him of his feelings of masculinity, and so his feelings for her are mixed. He may like to give in to his passive tendencies in her presence and to lean on her, but inwardly his feelings are not clear, for only under the most unusual circumstances could a man adopt a completely passive orientation without some negative psychological consequences.

Because so many incompatible things are demanded of the child by the overprotective mother, the chances are that his self-confidence will not be adequate. He is forced to be two people at the same time.

It is rather interesting that many achieving children have a feeling of unrest and disquietude when they are not busy. It is likely that the excessive linkage between the doting but demanding mother and the child is in part responsible for this (but other conditions must be met). In other words, a mother who is overly solicitous and who admires and expects a great deal from her child may produce these feelings of unrest. However, the mother of the underachiever demands a good bit more in addition; and her support is not as consistent and conflict-free as is the support of the achiever's mother. Where a mother is too-solicitous and expects a lot at the same time, there is a strong chance that the child will be restless unless he is accomplishing. However, a mother who in addition to being overly solicitous is also rejecting and irritable, is greatly demanding in terms of what the child "owes" her, is inclined to view the child as a self extension, and metes out affection in an erratic fashion—such a parent becomes the mother of an underachiever.

The child does not think of himself as a whole, unique, and independent person. He always wonders if he can do a job "well enough" (unconsciously, as well as mother could). In short, he is a psychological slave to an omnipresent ruler, whose commands he carries inside his head. He has located the source of evaluation of any action tendency in another nervous system (his mother's) instead of his own, and hence very few actions can be carried out in a nonconflicted, harmonious manner. This same phenomenon contributes to his sense of disquietude and feeling of restless incompleteness.

14.

Incompatible Parents

When the parents do not get along, the child's security is threatened. His personal sources of strength are failing him, and he may develop many negative reactions, one of which may be underachievement. The child depends on a stable adult world. He can imitate it, and thereby strengthen his inner resources. When he sees that his parents cannot tolerate each another, he loses a good bit of his faith and trust in the adult world in general, but in himself in particular.

Here are some ways in which a poor marital relation can affect a child's achievement.

1. The parents may use the child as a "pawn" in their battles. Some parents realize they have a bad marital relation but are afraid to recognize it. One or both parents may be dependent. When there is a fear of bringing the conflict out into the open, the child may be used as a substitute target of revenge. Each parent

may take out his or her own frustrations on the child. The mother may yell at the child when she really wants to yell at her husband. In addition, one or both may try to win over the child to a particular side. In these ways a subtle conflict may go on silently. There is no direct opposition between the parents, but there is a secret malignant force working on the child. This type of "secret" situation is every bit as bad as the one in which the parents argue out loud, screaming insults at one another.

2. When parents do argue out loud, very often the child's name will be mentioned. The child very often will blame himself for the conflict between his parents.

3. It is common for one parent to detest any trait in the child which resembles a trait in the hated spouse. The child may walk or talk or eat in a certain way, or do something else that reminds one of his parents of a similar trait in the mate. This embittered parent may punish its appearance in the child.

When a child perceives a split between his parents he becomes terrified. His school work may suddenly drop.

What is the child expressing by means of this poor school work? Any one or more of the following may be the answer:

1. The underachievement may be an unconscious scream of protest, carried out in an area in which the child hopes the parents will notice: school work.

2. The underachievement may be a demand that his parents cease hostilities and once more be sources of support.

3. The underachievement may represent the child's anxious demand that his parents reunite on the basis of his being in trouble. Many children realize that a common enemy (poor school work in this case) may cause two potential enemies (the mother and father) to reunite to make an allied attack on the common enemy.

4. The fourth point is the most general and is associated with all of the above. Underachievement reflects the child's drop in self-confidence and his anxious insecurity. The child wants to make these fears known to his parents, but for many reasons cannot communicate his fears openly.

Usually the underachievement reflects all of the above. It is the child's way of bringing his anxious concerns to the attention of his parents.

15

Parents Who Take Secret Pride in Their Child's Defiance

The Secret Delinquents

A recent finding in the field of juvenile delinquency is that a parent may take secret pride and pleasure in the fact that he has a defiant child. One of the child's parents (or both) is too inhibited to express his own angers and resentments to the important people with whom he associates. He is pleased that his child acts out defiant wishes as he would if he had more nerve. These parents do not realize they are unconsciously writing a "free ticket" for their child to be antisocial. On a conscious level this parent might imagine he is doing the opposite, that he is punishing and disciplining the child's behavior. Many such parents fail to do the very things that would lead to an improvement in the child's behavior. In like manner they do things to "help" the negative behavior last.

This parent senses unconsciously that underachievement has

defiant aspects. In one very real sense, underachievement *is* an act of defiance. The child renounces the social pressure which urges him to do good work.

The Subtle Program

What does this parent (usually the father) do to reinforce or help "stamp in" the defiant behavior? From the cases we have seen it is rather what he fails to do. For one thing, he fails to give the kind of warm encouragement that would be a positive aid to the child in his attempts to regain lost or slipping self-confidence.

On the other hand, he does do something actively. *He usually takes the side of the child against the school when this position is unwarranted.* The underachiever typically blames others for his own troubles. He is especially likely to blame his school and teachers. In such cases the majority of parents, while recognizing the child's right to complain, would gently side with the school—especially if there were no evidence to the contrary. The secretly defiant father sides with his child. He is telling the child: "You are right; authority is no good." The father is letting his child know that he can blame others—especially others in authority—for personal problems.

The Father versus the School

A variation on this situation is the one in which the father's pride becomes so involved with the problem that he adopts the attitude that the school *is* really to blame, and further, that he will "show them." This father is not primarily concerned with his child's poor work; he wants to win an argument. The father who cannot stand authority, who doubts his own self-confidence, and who has a fierce pride, will insist the school is to blame. The child is secondary; to "win the battle" is all important. He is most concerned with personal victory. This situation invariably ends up in the psychotherapist's office or else in an angry withdrawal of the child from the school—to everyone's detriment. Furthermore, by keeping his child's work at a poor level the father keeps his child a safe distance from himself intellectually. He makes sure the child will be no match for him.

Consequently the child thinks: "Why should I work harder or try to improve myself when the school is to blame. I know it is—Dad certainly thinks so."

Since such fathers (and occasionally mothers) do not fully realize what they are doing, psychotherapy or counseling is usually necessary in these cases. These parents must be shown how they are unwittingly sabotaging their children. Why should a child try to improve himself when his father has already told him his poor school work is not his own fault?

16.

The Boy Who Is Afraid
to Be a Sissy

The number of girl underachievers is low compared to the large number of boy underachievers. Girls develop optimal verbal abilities earlier than boys. Young boys are "by nature" at a disadvantage when competing with young girls in verbal areas. Girls find it easier and more agreeable to work within verbal media, like reading, writing, and spelling.

Many young boys think that learning itself is feminine. For one thing, learning is passive in the sense that the skeleton and the muscles are not called into play to any great extent, and "stronger muscles" is the main asset of the boy child. The process of learning, since it is part of general socialization, actually does appeal more to the (culturally and biologically) passive natures of girls than to the active natures of boys. When we use the word "passive" here, we refer to the fact that the muscular and skeletal systems are not used extensively; learning is not, we repeat *not*, psychologically a passive experience—at least it shouldn't be.

Another thing: most elementary school teachers are women. It is no wonder, then, that young boys think of the process of learning as being on the "feminine" side.

These facts do not make much difference to the majority of boys. But suppose we run into a boy who is afraid of being a sissy. Since he secretly fears he is feminine, he is extra sensitive to anything which seems even remotely "girlish." To this boy, learning my be a psychological threat. It threatens his feelings of masculinity and hence his entire sense of identity.

In some cases the fear of being feminine is so intense that the fear is not only a "contributing cause" but the main cause of the underachievement. This boy usually emphasizes masculine activities. Aside from being an underachiever, he may become a bully as well. He may shove others around in an additional attempt to convince himself he harbors no inner passivity.

One of the toughest and most pugnacious characters we have ever met was such a boy. He was initially referred to us because he had very poor marks in the high school he attended and was forever in fights, bullying younger children. This boy was actually "delicate" and "passive" on the inside. He had an appreciation for fine art work and, more important, had very submissive fantasies in which he played the role of a slave. He had, in addition, the characteristics of a passive and "weak" person. But outwardly he would not tolerate the idea of being passive or feminine. He would never admit to his interest in fine arts. He was forever in trouble with the police or with the school authorities. He stole automobiles, ruined the products his salesman-father stored in the garage, and on one occasion ruined the family's small boat. He made fun of school and played the role of the bully. He tried to hide the submissive part of his personality from everyone, especially from himself.

The major "cure" in this area consists of understanding why the boy feels sensitive about his nature and then by reducing the conflicts which gave rise to the sensitivity. This type of problem generally requires the attention of a professionally trained psychotherapist. Such fears usually engender more complex reactions than underachievement.

17

The Spoiled Child

Underachievement is only one of many things which may result from "spoiling." We are interested in the "spoiled child" only if he is additionally an underachieving child.

The Difference between the Overprotected Child and the Spoiled Child

A separate category should be reserved for those children who are "spoiled" but not necessarily overprotected.

Remember, it is not the mere doing of too much or of being overly solicitous that characterizes an overprotective mother. The overprotective mother has definite psychological conflicts, and her overconcern for her child is but one symptom of these conflicts.

What then happens to the child who has otherwise conflict-free relatives who just plain do too much for him? We speak in the plural here, for it is usually a family that "spoils" a child. If it were one person alone who did the "spoiling," we would probably be dealing with an overprotective person, and the word "spoiled" would be too mild to describe the situation.

This chapter deals largely with the child who is an only child in an overadmiring family. No one person spends too much time doing things for him, but because of the sheer number of interested persons the child hardly ever has a chance to do things for himself. By the time all the relatives get a chance to do their bit for the child, all of the child's waking time has been consumed. No *one* relative is anxiously concerned; there are just so many of them.

When this situation exists, two rather negative things may happen.

1. If the child really becomes "spoiled," in the popular sense of the word, he rarely learns to exert himself in a consistent fashion. Why should he? Good accomplishment takes effort, even in the early grades. The school requires a certain degree of conformity. The child has not been prepared to meet these requirements. He has always had other people ready to serve him, very often anticipating and meeting his every need. Not only did a host of admiring relatives meet his every demand, but there were even times when his needs were met before he fully knew he had them.

The spoiled child may not be prepared to meet his teacher even half way. He *may* do acceptable work in the early grades, provided he is bright, since a minimum of effort is generally required of the very bright child in the early grades. Sooner or later, however, his unwillingness to exert himself or to apply himself with any consistency will catch up with him. When things are taught which he does not "catch" easily, he will fall behind.

2. The birth of a younger sibling is reacted to by this child as if it were a major catastrophe. The birth of a younger sibling is bound to produce difficulty in any family, but the previously spoiled child reacts as if his entire world was uprooted and destroyed. The spoiled child upon the birth of a sibling will lose his position of magnified importance in the family (although very

likely he may in reality still be the favorite). In his own mind he will experience this event as a disaster. The variety of personality reconfigurations which may now occur are beyond our present scope. In general, when the spoiled child is faced with a new sibling, the situation should be handled just the way one would handle the appearance of a sibling in any family situation. If a new sibling enters the life of the particularly spoiled child at just that point when the child is entering school or when school work is becoming extra-difficult, this spoiled child's reaction is likely to be intense. His achievement may falter to a marked degree. The child may feel his parents have betrayed him, will harbor great amounts of resentment against the new child, and in general will feel his life has taken a tragic turn. In addition to treating the underachievement in this case, one must also treat the effects of the appearance of a new and hated rival.

18.

Situational Causes of Temporary
Underachievement

Psychological factors do not always play the prime role in underachievement. Even though they are obviously at work in all instances, the cases we are going to speak about now do not usually require any direct psychological treatment.

Underachievement is described as situational or temporary if the underachievement is taking place in a child who is free of serious and debilitating underlying emotional conflicts. It is called situational not because it is set in motion by any particular or definite situation, but because the child is essentially free of conflict, and will therefore improve as his immediate surroundings change either in actuality or in the way he views them. For example, suppose a child changes homes, and the strangeness of the new home frightens him and causes his grades to drop. If he is essentially conflict-free, his grades will improve as he begins to feel more at home in his new surroundings. If this same thing happens to a conflicted child it may become the first notable event or trigger in a more serious and chronic problem.

In this chapter we are concerned with temporary underachievement caused by: (1) A change in schools (or neighborhood), (2) A teacher who picks on the child, (3) Other children who pick on the child, (4) A neighborhood that discourages learning, (5) Temporary failure in one particular subject.

(Another case is that of the extremely bright child who is so bored by the regular routine of the class that his attention wanders and the quality of his work appears to be poor.)

A Change in Schools

Lionel was a young boy who had always done well in school. His father had to change jobs when Lionel was in the fifth grade. The new job was in a new city. When Lionel entered the new school he felt out of place. He felt like an unaccepted stranger. The teaching methods were different. Nothing seemed familiar to him. He did not feel at home during recess or at lunchtime. His work slipped.

Our first approach was to find out whether or not Lionel had significant emotional conflicts—conflicts so intense as to prevent him from developing self-confidence in his new surroundings. The psychological tests revealed no evidence of significant conflict. Therefore Lionel's difficulties were considered situational and temporary. We figured that when Lionel no longer perceived himself as a stranger in an alien environment, he would change for the better. The important thing really was that in our opinion this would happen on its own—no psychological treatment would be necessary. If Lionel had had serious underlying conflicts, the chances are that he would have been hopelessly behind by the time he felt more "accepted." We recommended brief tutoring in the particular subjects in which Lionel was doing the most poorly to speed up Lionel's "recovery."

The tutoring was initiated in order to guard against the possibility of having a temporary setback change into a major setback (which is possible though not probable in a basically conflict-free child). We felt it was important to bring the boy up to date on those things he had missed during the time he was experiencing a temporary loss of self-confidence.

A change in schools or a change in neighborhoods may produce a temporary condition of underachievement. In such cases, as in all cases, the first thing to do is to determine the probable causes of the underachievement. It is crucial to find out whether or not there are any serious underlying emotional conflicts within the child's personality.

When a Teacher Picks on the Child

Once in a while your child may run into a teacher who picks on him. This will of course make the child feel uncomfortable in school. The child's work is likely to slip. This can be considered a situational cause of underachievement if it is felt the child's work will automatically improve when he leaves this particular classroom, or if the child's personality is not so brittle as to be more permanently impaired by this noxious encounter.

If the child can present reasonably good evidence that the teacher does pick on him, a talk with that teacher is in order. If this does not help things, a talk with the principal is next. It is usually not good to "down" the teacher too much or to overly side with the child against the teacher, even if the teacher is wrong. The parents should proceed in a matter-of-fact way to explain to the child that once in a while his teachers may not be very fair, but this is indeed the exceptional case. The child should not be made to feel that any time he gets in difficulty he can "pass the buck" to his current teacher. He would be inclined to do so if too much "righteous indignation" is expended about the teacher. In addition, the child will begin to feel very negative about schools. The parents should matter-of-factly acknowledge that sometimes two people will not hit it off well, and that they as his parents will try to set things right. The parents should then talk with the teacher and perhaps the principal. If the child's work has slipped too much, tutoring should be initiated in the particular subjects in which he has fallen behind. It is not likely that a talk with the teacher will cause miraculous changes in this teacher's feelings for the child. The teacher will likely be hurt and insulted. If there is no change on the part of the teacher, the child should be reassigned to another class. If this is not possible, the child should be given warm understanding at home, but not in an overly dramatic fashion. He should be encouraged to keep up with his work even though his teacher is "perhaps unfair." If the child's work does not improve when he moves on from the "traumatic" teacher's class, it would be wise to seek professional advice. Again, as in other cases, the procedure would be to see if the tests show any evidence of deep psychological conflicts. Educational tutoring may be necessary if he is too far behind in certain subjects.

Jimmy complained his teacher was always "on his back." She yelled at him and blamed him for everything. He felt quite uncomfortable in class. As the term wore on, his work gradually fell from an A to a D level. By the end of the term it was obvious that Jimmy's work was poor. When we saw Jimmy, we felt his poor work was due to the fact he was picked on in school; the psychological tests revealed no serious emotional conflicts. The parents were advised to talk things over with the teacher. The parents were not encouraged to malign the teacher, even though likely the teacher was to blame. Jimmy was given warm encouragement and minimal significance was assigned to his school difficulties. Jimmy was promoted to the next grade. He entered the next grade with renewed self-confidence because of the warm encouragement given to him by his parents and by us. He was able to lift his work to its previous high level.

Once in a while a child is so hurt by being picked on that his work goes down and stays down. When this happens, we generally find a pre-existing sensitivity in the child. In these cases, psychological treatment, sometimes of a short-term nature, is indicated.

A child should never be told: "Oh, but the teacher really likes you," if this is not true. It is far more sensible to show and convince the child that some people will *not* like him, and that this state of affairs is no catastrophe.

Many people are inclined to explain underachievement strictly in terms of that which brings it to light or makes it noticeable for the first time. Some people assume that underachievement is caused by the triggering condition. These misled people are amazed that the underachievement lasts even when the triggering events have changed radically. They make the same mistake as someone who would try to understand the entire phenomenon of light by understanding what makes the "off and on" switch work. Consider the case of the boy who is developing inwardly like the typical underachiever. He has lost his self-confidence, feels his entire sense of self worth depends upon his ability to achieve, and has a drastic fear of failure. He runs into a teacher who picks on him. The cycle is set into motion. From a potential underachiever, he becomes an actual underachiever. In this case the underachievement is not temporary or situational. A preexisting tendency was set off by what appeared on the surface to be a temporary thing. Parents are inclined to ignore underachievement if they think its cause is temporary. Parents should not rush to consult the psychologist at the first sign of below-average work; we do mean to emphasize the trouble that follows from confusing a trigger with an entire mechanism.

When Children Pick on the Child

A child may be very unpopular in school. Other children may pick on him. If this happens, it is difficult for the child to find school agreeable or enjoyable. The child will be tense during class. His work will probably suffer. It is usually difficult to get a child to admit that other children are bothering him in school. It makes him feel like a sissy. Should parents notice their child expressing dislike or disgust for school, it would be wise for them to find out if other children are picking on him. If they are, they should consult the principal. In some cases it is possible for the principal to stop these unfair practices. Should the parents decide to consult the school, they should proceed with a great deal of tact. If the child is made to feel like an inept sissy who cannot fight his own battles, more harm than good will be done. The parents should tell the child that children who are bullies are nuisances and *should* be reported to the principal. They should make the child know they are reporting the bullies not because these children happen to be picking on him, but because as bullies they should be reported. The parents should let the child know they are not fighting his battles, but rather are performing a public service. A school's purpose is to teach. When the school cannot do its job because of rowdy children, they should be quieted. Naturally the parents should use discretion in labeling a "bully." The rough-and-ready dominant youngster is not necessarily a bully. But when a chronic, organized, and systematic assault is launched against one single child by another child or by a group of other children, adult intervention is warranted.

The Neighborhood That Discourages Learning

If you live in a neighborhood that collectively feels education is for sissies, you are in a relatively difficult situation. It will be difficult for you as parents to value education in your home without producing some degree of conflict within the child. If your child's school work falls because he is afraid that if he were to study the other children would make fun of him, it is difficult to straighten things out. Most parents try to convince the child to ignore his boorish friends. They tell the child school work is more important than the friends he happens to have at the moment. However, it is one thing for the parents, from their position of security, to tell the child this, and another thing for the child to do anything about it. After all, the child spends a good deal of time with his peers, and their feelings are very important to him.

If talking to the child does not do the trick, then most parents find it necessary either to change neighborhoods or to enroll the child in a private school. In some communities it is possible to shift the child from one school to another, although most public schools do not favor this course of action.

Once in a while it is possible to work out difficulties like this through neighborhood community councils or PTA's. However, it has been our experience that when the children of a community devalue education, the parents of these children do the same thing, usually covertly or unconsciously. Even though the parents may give lip service to the necessity of an education, there is usually no "push" behind this lip service. When the community devalues education, the PTA approach is usually fruitless.

Another approach is to have some interested and talented parent form a hobby group or some other sort of group to which the neighborhood children can become attached. This admired parent can gradually begin a campaign to stress accomplishment and the pursuit of excellence. These ideals are often very hard to meet "in the field." A neighborhood which thoroughly devalues education is a rather formidable opponent for the parent who is interested in educational excellence.

The idealistic ways of handling such community problems (forming study groups through community organizations like PTA's, etc.) are unfortunately not very practical. Rather glumly we report the "majority solution" to this problem involves a change in neighborhoods or a change in schools. Group psychotherapy with "key" children holds out promise as a constructive maneuver. The authors have recently initiated such activity. Results are promising, but it is too soon to reach definite conclusions.

Failure in One Particular Subject

Very often a child may have extreme difficulty with one particular subject. When this happens, his self-confidence may be upset. His work in all areas may be affected. It is generally advisable to begin educational tutoring when the child appears to have *definite* trouble with a subject. Tutoring should not only serve to help him in the particular area in which he is doing poorly, but also should help guard against a complete failure in self-confidence. For if this poor work lasts too long, the child's entire self-confidence may be affected, and you will then have more than a temporary or situational problem on your hands. The idea here is to prevent a situational condition from becoming a more permanent state.

Again, discretion is called for. Before the parents take any action, they should make sure a child is really having difficulty. If they are not cautious it will appear to the child that his parents are anxiously overconcerned with accomplishment. We generally advise the parents to use the following signs to determine when to take action:

1) if the child himself complains of difficulty with some subject for more than one month (and the situation does not respond to usual parental aid).

2) if the child does failing work which remains at this level for more than one third of a given school term.

3) if a child's grade in a particular subject is *consistently* and markedly lower than the rest of his grades (though not necessarily at a failing level).

If any of these conditions is met, tutoring is warranted, followed by a regular diagnostic procedure, should this prove necessary.

These situations need not be thought of as underachievement.

However, sometimes what starts out as a mild reaction changes into a major calamity. There have been cases where mild situational disabilities have gradually changed into major cases of underachievement. The child begins with a mild reaction. In one particular case, the child was protesting the fact that his parents did not give him a bicycle. Although he did not make the conscious decision to retaliate, soon afterward his work began to slip. It seemed just on the threshold of his awareness that he was angry at his parents for their oversight, and that he was getting even by allowing the quality of his school work to slip. However, while he was in his protest stage he apparently missed some crucial work in school. When he wanted to do better, and tried, he found he was already far behind and did not possess the necessary information to do better. Now he was really worried. From this point, his difficulties with school subjects increased and he became more and more like the typical underachiever. His parents were made anxious by his now continuously failing work and began to yell at him. He gradually came to feel they loved him only if he could do excellent work. This ushered in a close parallel to the typical underachievement process. Luckily the child was brought to the attention of the appropriate professional persons and the problem was solved early. However, do not draw the conclusion that parents should satisfy all of the whims and wants of their children or else they will be faced with underachievement.

When a child's grades slip for a single term, and this is due to an obvious situational stress, or due to the child's desire to prove a point, the child should not be labeled an underachiever. If the parents become overly concerned with what is a passing trifle, they stand to do more harm than good. What starts out as a situational problem *can* become a more serious problem. If the child's grades stay down even though he seems to really try his best, if he actively complains he cannot understand what is being taught in school, if what started out as a temporary slipping seems to be turning into a permanent situation, action should be taken. There are many potential courses of action. The first should be a discussion with the teacher, followed by an individual psychological examination. If there is no evidence of emotional conflict noted in the psychological tests, tutoring is indicated. If there is evidence of conflict, psychotherapy may also be indicated.

19.

The Bright but
Bored Child

Ralph was brought to us because his school work was poor. His parents were surprised: Ralph always seemed bright at home. He spoke well at an early age, finding it easy to learn and use new words. His parents were shocked and amazed when they noticed Ralph was not doing good work in school. His work was quite good in the first grade and acceptable in the second grade. Its quality began to slip in the third grade, and by the time Ralph reached fourth grade his work was inferior, although he was not failing any subject. Psychological tests revealed that Ralph had superior intelligence. They further revealed he could appropriately handle arithmetic, writing, reading, and all other school subjects. Upon investigation it became apparent that Ralph was bored in school. He went on to form bad habits early in the game. First-grade work was so easy for Ralph that he completed his assignments in a relatively short time. His attention then wandered. Before long he ceased paying attention in school completely, and eventually he did not even understand what was going on in class. At this point his work slipped.

What happened to Ralph is common in our classrooms. Most bright children can, however, re-adapt themselves to the class program. If the classroom routine is not stimulating, they invent little things of their own to do and to think about. In this way they maintain their interest in the work. The crucial point is this: Successfully bright children stay attuned to the school program even though they may "enrich" it in their own inner worlds.

Marvin was an eight-year-old boy in the third grade. His teachers called him a "dreamer." He was forever sitting around drawing pictures of rocket ships. A trained eye would have spotted an active fantasy life. Marvin never seemed to pay attention in class. His first-grade teacher had told his third-grade teacher that Marvin was an exceptionally bright student, but the third-grade teacher doubted the verity of this judgment, as had his second-grade teacher. Marvin's work had begun to slip in the second grade and now in the third grade was no longer acceptable.

We examined Marvin and found he had superior native intelligence. After the tests were interpreted and scored it became obvious that his inefficiency in school was due to boredom. Since the school system Marvin was in had no accelerated classes and his parents could not afford a special school for him (where the work could, potentially at least, be geared to his abilities) it was necessary to plan a program that would help him gain a greater interest in what he was doing.

Sometimes a child has such a bright and fertile mind that he finds it almost impossible to proceed at what to him is a snail's pace. He is bored when forced to work at the level found comfortable by the other children in the class. A child like Ralph belongs in a school situation geared to the needs of the exceptionally bright child. Many school systems recognize this problem and cope with it successfully. Many cities have special classes and/or schools for children like Ralph. Parents who think their child belongs in a special situation usually arrange for the child to take psychological tests. The tests are given either by a school psychologist or by a clinical psychologist. Parents who think their child belongs in this type of special situation should contact their school guidance counselor. Sometimes it is not practical to have the child change schools or be admitted to a special class. When this is the case, there are a number of things the parents can do to help the bright but bored child. They can encourage him to read ahead in his books but to keep abreast of what is going on in class. The parents can suggest ways for the child to enrich the regular class material by thinking of peripheral material on his own. The bright child can be urged to cover the area in more depth than the other children.

This approach can be used in other subjects as well. The child should be encouraged to remain attuned to what is going on in his classrom so that he will not fall behind or cause a disturbance in class.

The best thing to do with the bright but bored child is to put him in the school situation which can best meet his individual needs, e.g., small classes, individual attention, and so on. If this is not possible, the thing to do is to teach him to use the current school program as a taking-off point to which he can add all sorts of interesting details of his own. There is only one thing to guard against. It is imperative that the bright child be convinced not to "depart" from the school program too far or for too long. He should not lose track of what is going on in the class. This becomes increasingly important in the higher grades. Bright children often find it easy to function efficiently in the early grades. No specific studying is usually called for. Most class work involves basic reading, writing, and arithmetic. The bright child could probably function efficiently in these areas even before he entered school. He probably learned how to read, how to write, and probably how to do simple arithmetic. However, in the higher grades more and more specific content knowledge is called for. There is no way for the bright child to acquire this knowledge other than by reading and studying the assignments given to him. The problem cannot be worked out by mere "intelligence" alone, but require specific knowledge.

We encourage the child to stay abreast of his work. He should be taught to view what is being taught to him in a more complicated and all-encompassing light than would be possible for the other children. If he does this, he will stay attuned to what is being taught, but at the same time will elaborate on it in a manner more suitable to his intelligence. He can be taught to relate what he learns in history, for example, to what he learns in current events. He can be taught to relate what he learns in arithmetic to many concrete problems in life, while at the same time he can be encouraged to understand the basically abstract nature of mathematics. This type of broad thinking can furnish pleasing and satisfying experiences.

20.

The Mixed Sociologic-
Neurotic Case

In most cases of underachievement the child has internalized or made his own the conviction that good achievement is desirable, but other parts of his personality neurotically oppose this conviction.

However, in some instances the parents only superficially value education, and are really disinterested or even actually opposed to it.

In some cases where the child may seem a neurotic underachiever, he is really responding to his parents' actual, just-below-the-surface anti-educational values. Usually, there are mixed neurotic elements in such cases.

Mario S., aged eleven, the oldest of four brothers, was referred to us because of poor school grades. His marks were acceptable in the early grades, but gradually got worse over the years. When we first saw him, he was in the sixth grade, where he was failing three of his four major subjects.

Mario's father had taken over a fading out-of-state fruit business and by hard work built a flourishing corporation. Although he lacked a formal education, having quit school at a young age, he was an industrious man and became financially successful. Knowing how hard he had had to work, he wanted Mario to have a fine education and an easier life than he.

Mario admitted early in our work with him that although his marks were low, he really cared not a fig. Many underachieving children appear nonchalant on the surface, admitting they care very little for school. However, the majority of them inwardly do care, but are afraid to commit themselves to hard work. Our first thought was that Mario was also afraid to try, or was rebelling against parental pressure by doing poor school work.

However, a different story soon unfolded. Mario's parents, although superficially urging Mario to do good work in school, really saw education as a status symbol more than anything else. In fact, Mario's father really distrusted education. He knew he had "made it" without one, and so did Mario. Lip service was paid to education, but little more than that. And so Mario was actually internalizing his father's real sense of values, which was not far from the surface: he was not for but against education. This antieducational bias was not initially a neurotically determined attitude in Mario's case (nor, apparently in his father's) but a social one. Mario's father came from an area where a good education was suspect. It was not considered "good" to have an education.

Although there were a few neurotic or conflicted elements in this case, we dealt here with essentially a sociologic cause of underachievement posing as a neurotic one. Education was really not valued by Mario's father, and there was nothing wrong with Mario when he correctly interpreted his father's true underlying attitude.

Cases which thus rest mainly on antieducational values should be distinguished from cases in which the poor school grades rest on conflicted emotional attitudes. Although in practice these extremes are rarely found in pure form, it is important to determine which cause predominates, since the treatment and prognosis is different in the two conditions. The prognosis is usually more negative in a case like Mario's, since the boy really feels no push to change himself. It is actually easier to remove a neurotic inhibition than it is to "build in" a value which has been absent during the crucial formative years. When this type of sociological case is met, the therapist usually encourages the child to identify with him (the therapist) and gradually adopt the therapist's educational values. This is not the same treatment route followed with other, more neurotic cases.

21.

Underachievement Associated with More Serious Underlying Problems

Underachievement may be a side effect of almost any serious emotional disturbance. Any neurosis, psychosis, character disturbance, or other form of pathology may produce underachievement. Any person who thus becomes an underachiever may or may not have the more typical underachiever traits. It is also possible that an underachiever may be doing poorly because he has both some core traits *and* a more serious disturbance.

Underachievement may be a symptom of a relatively minor neurotic condition that could improve with minimal treatment, but it may also be a symptom of a developing psychotic condition. Sometimes underachievement will be the first identifiable sign of a more serious problem. For these reasons it is important that underachievers be evaluated by professionally competent people. As mentioned, the diagnostic procedure for the underachiever is a broad one, and this is rightly so. What appears to be a mild case of underachievement may turn out to be a more serious thing. This is, of course, the exceptional case, but it is one that should be considered for the sake of completeness.

Some children form the irrational assumption, which becomes deeply entrenched in their personalities, that they cannot "exist" and function in the absence of a great deal of parental support and benevolence. Such a child feels he must adopt *all* the values and commandments of some highly valued adult. He rarely adopts a "compromise" solution, i.e., the approach that allows him to adopt *most* of this valued adult's wishes. Rather he feels he must think and act in accordance with *all* of the adult's explicit and implicit commands. But to do this would mean the complete submergence of his own personality. And so a serious trap is set: he can either act in accordance with *all* the valued adult's commands and allow his own personality to be annihilated in the process, or he can try to disown completely the valued adult's "commandments."

Some children caught in this trap become complete rebels and throw away pro-school values. These children have equated an acceptance of school with total surrender to the valued adult and the consequent annihilation of their own personalities. To guard against this possibility, they may disown *all* of the ambivalently experienced "commands," feeling they must do so or else lose their own identities. To this type of child, school stands for a submergence and annihilation of identity. This type of condition would require long-term psychotherapy.

The diagnostic procedure should include a medical examination and possibly neurologic or psychiatric examinations, as well as complete psychological and educational evaluations. It is important to rule out the possibility of somatic pathology, just as it is of crucial importance to identify the exact psychological causes operative in each case.

Very often the child who has a nagging suspicion there is something seriously the matter within his personality will "slow down" his psychological pace. This type of defensive constriction was first described by Dr. Zygmunt A. Piotrowski some years ago (in relation to a serious type of emotional disturbance). The child unconsciously and/or consciously senses that his thoughts and feelings are chaotic, confused, and perhaps panic-producing. He may experience intense feelings of loneliness or "distance" from others. He may feel "unreal." He sees that his judgments are quite often at odds with those of others, and that when he follows them he gets into difficulty. But he realizes that to "ac- acomplish" he must exert himself and depend on these disturbed personality functions. He then senses that if he exerts himself, his already strained personality will be pushed to a critical limit. He also fears his defective reasoning and judgment will be mani- fested to himself and to those around him. He adopts a defensive cautiousness.

The child who is pushed into this form of defensive constriction may appear slow and dull to others. His school work will prob- ably suffer to a large extent. It is important that this type of defensive caution be recognized for what it is. This is done by means of psychological personality tests, particularly projective tests like the Rorschach. Of course not all children who appear slow and dull are defensively constricted. Again we see the im- portance of having a thorough study made of the child who is doing poorly in school. If the underachievement is but one symp- tom of a more serious underlying problem, the psychologist will recommend an appropriate treatment program. The underachieve- ment will be treated as a secondary symptom and dealt with in its proper time.

PART TWO

Recommendations
for Action

22.

Some Preliminary
Remarks

One aim of this book is to furnish the parent with some insight into why he or she may be doing certain negative things. We are further interested in making some recommendations we feel will help change the underachiever into an achiever.

Often a parent knows what could be done to make the child more comfortable, more confident, and more efficient. Somehow or other the things are not done. These parents cannot get themselves out of their "ruts." It is very hard to break habits; and it is almost impossible to break them without understanding at least some of the reasons they are held with such tenacity.

We do not intend to provide a list of do's and don'ts which can be uncritically applied. When we mention a "do" or a "don't" it will be accompanied by an explanation, and the understanding of the explanation will prove of greater importance than the "do" or "don't" itself. There is little staying power behind a gimmick.

This is why the majority of books of study habits cannot really help an underachiever. Underachievement is caused by emotional conflict. It is not caused by having a lightbeam shine over the wrong shoulder, or by the child's not devoting an exactly proper number of minutes to studying. Since it is a result of conflicted emotional attitudes, only a readjustment of attitudes will be of lasting help.

23.

How to Get the Child Interested
in Good Achievement

Setting the Stage

We consider healthy self-confidence to be more "important" insofar as learning is concerned than the particular study methods used. If self-confidence is poor, study "habits" would be of little use. Keep in mind that we refer to the child's confidence in himself as an achieving person. We do not refer to the confidence he may or may not have in his relations with relatives, peers, and so forth.

This section of the book will be concerned with ways to change the underachiever into an achiever. Many things we mention are things to not do. Most children are born with healthy, assertive, curiosity. If the child cannot make use of these natural talents, it is because he has been somehow "beaten down." Consequently, to restore an underachiever to his naturally assertive, confident, and inquisitive state, we must concentrate on eliminating the negative and hampering conditions that have been imposed upon him. There is, however, one "positive" thing to be done.

Getting the Child Interested in Good Achievement

Most children have inborn assertive curiosity. If the basically sound child does not have this trait, something has been or is inhibiting this natural "talent." Aside from teaching the underachiever optimal study methods, there is one positive sequence of behavior which will "produce" an achiever. Two conditions must be met. *The parents must provide an "intellectual," assertively curious atmosphere in the home.* But additionally, *the child must like and admire these parents enough to identify with and thereby imitate them.* Neither condition alone is as powerful as the two in combination. To round out this program, the parents should gently emphasize pleasure in the work itself, and de-emphasize the doing of good work to please, flatter, or gain affection from the parents. The child should come to enjoy the work or performance itself, and not any psychological reward resulting from it (like parental praise).

Parents should be alert and interested in things. They should value accomplishment themselves, but *not directly pressure* the child to do the same. The most effective teacher makes the child want to imitate him, not through pressure but through admiration. The child not only becomes fascinated with the work itself but wants to gain praise and recognition from this admired teacher. The child wants to be admitted to what he considers the radiant company of his teacher—or parents, if they set the example. The child discovers the ticket of entrance to this company is knowledge and the ability to hold his own in a lively conversation. He tackles the job of acquiring this knowledge. He does it with no ambivalence or conflict because the teachers (the parents) have not made him feel he will be unloved if he fails. He wants to join his "teacher" (intellectually), and so is motivated to a good work. The more a child likes and admires his parents, the more he wants to imitate them. The more he dislikes them, or the more the unreasonable demands made of him, the less he wants to (consciously) copy them. (He may copy, or identify with, their undesirable traits.)

The Positive Approach

If a positive atmosphere is provided, the child will naturally imitate what he admires. If the child is pressured to live this kind of life, he will resist. But the child should feel challenged intellectually by his parents. The point is that he not feel *ordered to produce*. The parents should convey by words and actions the fun involved in intellectual attainment. If the parents are themselves dull people who depend on "passive" media like movies or television as the sole means of entertainment, and sit around without talking or without reflective thought, there is no reason to expect the child to be different. The child *may perhaps* be different, but to expect this under such dull conditions would involve risk. Children copy and imitate what they see. There is an old saying some parents tell their children: "Do not do as I do, but do as I say." This rarely works. Children, especially bright children, will not do as they are told, but rather will do as they see. If a child does not see his parents as bright and alert people, no matter what they order or tell him verbally, he will probably not be a bright and alert achiever. (There are some few exceptions to this. The child with dull parents may encounter some other bright achieving adult person, become psychologically attached to that person, and seek to imitate him. Why, however, depend on such a chance event?)

The most effective teachers never pressure children into learning things. They merely act alertly themselves. They are knowledgeable in the subjects they teach. Their students admire them and try to copy them. The child should be encouraged *to be interested in the concrete work or performance itself, and not in some psychological reaction resulting from it, like affection or praise from parents.*

Specifically, here are some things parents could do.

When the child is young, the parents, particularly the mother, should help the child develop a strong and well-rounded vocabulary. The mother should help the child attach correct verbal labels to things around him. Baby talk should be avoided. She should encourage his attempts to gain verbal mastery and understanding of the objects and events in his surroundings. This should be done in a relatively quiet, nonrigid manner. The child should not be tested, such as by the mother's saying, "Now what do we call this?" and then following with an angry exclamation should the child fail the "test." A sound vocabulary furnishes the foundation for future learning. A general rule is to explain things and events to a child beforehand, and follow the encounters with discussions. It is important to not "talk down" to the child.

Parents should take their children on trips, and talk about things they have read. When they watch television programs they should discuss their contents. There is nothing wrong with movies or TV provided they are approached in an *active* and alert manner. Parents should relate what they see and hear to things they already know, and should invite the child to join such activity. They should have lively discussions about things the child will encounter in the future. A bright inquisitive parent will question what he sees. He will relate new information to knowledge he already possesses. If a so-called "true life" TV program defies his background of knowledge, he will say so. In addition, he may attempt to relate current events shown on TV to historical events. He will try to show how today's news grows from past events.

Curiosity is already there in "bud" form, and will emerge when parents set appropriate examples. An important point: Such a program must be carried out in a relaxed, nonpushing manner. Some readers may feel these programs unnecessary. One could probably name many bright and creative geniuses who had dull, sadistic, or uninterested parents. Our point is it is a risk to expect a child to be a good achiever under negative conditions. That there are historical exceptions does not surprise us. However, one recent author, Bernice Eiduson, in the book, *Scientists: Their Psychological World* (N.Y.: Basic Books, 1962) asserted that many very bright and creative persons reported miserable early lives when this was untrue. She felt many of these people actually had a need to think they had unhappy childhoods. So even "historical exceptions" are difficult to evaluate.

Some perfectionistic adults cannot tolerate silliness. Such a parent feels silly behavior ruins things. This misguided parent may be having an "intellectual" discussion with his child when the child suddenly becomes "silly." The parent thinks: "Now why did the child have to ruin things? We were having a good time before he became so silly." The parent becomes annoyed and criticizes the child. The discussion is ended, each participant having been "wounded" in the process. Instead of having allowed the child to have his moment of random silliness, the parent became annoyed, and the child was made uncomfortable.

There is also the parent who cannot stand the thought of the child having a bright and independent opinion. He or she unconsciously fears the child's assertive behavior and puts a damper on any independent thinking. No matter what the child's idea might be, this parent must prove it inferior to one of his own.

It is not true that pain supplies the only effective motivation in life. It is a myth that bright and productive people must have neurotic and "sick" childhoods. Pleasure and competitively tinged pleasure are also powerful motivating forces. Too bad most parents do not take advantage of this ancient knowledge.

24

The Child's Right
to Be Himself

The Fear of Anger

It is likely that the mother or father (or both) of a passive-aggressive child is frightened by anger in the child and inhibits its expression in any form. When the parent sees anger in his own child, it brings three fearful possibilities to mind. It reminds him of the anger he felt or feels toward his own parents and this ushers in feelings of guilt. Few people like to be reminded of parent-directed anger. For another thing, the parent believes his own child may feel toward him the way he secretly feels about his own parents. We are using the father in our example, but this applies equally to mothers. He fears his own child may secretly resent him, just as part of his own personality resents his parents. Thirdly, he fears even mild anger will force him to lose control of himself—that he may be carried away by an onslaught of retaliatory rage. He fears his capacity for self-control is inadequate to the potential strength of his rage.

The next case illustrates some of these fears in a mother.

Rita was the mother of a first-grader, Betty. Betty, an only child, was fearful, whining, and demanding; she was unable to learn her first-grade work. Rita was a good mother in most respects, but she had a good bit of semirepressed resentment against her own mother. Rita recognized that her current relation with this mother was a confused one. Rita felt overly attached to her mother in an unusual way. She felt everything she did had to reflect glory on her mother, please her, or flatter her. She went out of her way to impress her mother, and yet at the same time did not really enjoy her mother's company. She resented the fact that her mother was such a powerful motivating force in her life. She resented having to adjust her own life to her mother's. She resented the fact that her mother's evaluations of her actions were more important to her than her own. She wanted admiration and praise from her mother, except that her desires were insatiable and unrealistic. Rita wanted Betty, her own little girl, to be perfect so that her mother (the child's grandmother) would be impressed by Rita's child-rearing abilities. Unconsciously she wanted to prove she was the better mother. Thus Betty's potential perfection represented an aggressively competitive demonstration of superiority. Also on an unconscious level was prior hostility Rita felt toward Betty. For with Betty's birth Rita's sense of identity changed from that of a daughter to that of a mother. Unconsciously Rita feared independence—part of her personality wanted to remain a protected daughter. With Betty's birth, Rita no longer could (unconsciously) think of herself as a "daughter." She was now a mother.

Before psychotherapy allowed her to resolve these conflicts, she tried to ignore them. However, she developed a conviction that her own little girl, Betty, hated her. She made of Betty an "enemy." Periodically Rita was overcome by guilt, and so her approach became inconsistent, varying between hateful rejection and guilty "love." Any anger in Betty threatened to bring to mind Rita's resentments of her own mother, and her underlying anger at Betty herself, who forced her identity to change from that of daughter to mother. Also when Rita looked at her daughter, she felt she was resented, just as she "secretly" resented her own mother. She would not tolerate anger in Betty. When these fears and conflicts were communicated to Betty, the roots were planted for a future underachievement problem.

The first and most general suggestion is that each parent think over how he or she has been acting toward the underachieving child. Recall how you act when the child is angry. Are you consistently irritated, and do you overreact? Do you fly into a rage yourself? Do you shower him with endearments? Do you give him long speeches about being "nice"? Do you tell him it is evil to be angry at others? Remember: a child should feel free to feel angry, although he should not be allowed to physically hit or attack younger siblings. When the child is in a critical mood, this should not be taken as "talking back in a fresh manner." Gradually as the child grows older, say by the age of three, he should be reminded he is entitled to feel angry, but that this does not mean he should necessarily yell about it or be openly defiant. In this way, the child is given the freedom to feel angry, but is taught he may not express this anger in any way he pleases. Some parents worry about giving a child too much freedom. However, it is better to make a mistake on the side of freedom than on the side of hampering restriction, *especially when it concerns the freedom to have emotional feelings.* Far more damage is done by inhibiting the very young child than by allowing him to feel free to express resentment. He must be taught to respect the rights of others when respect is appropriate. Of course he can be encouraged to stand up for his own rights—by physical force if necessary—when this is appropriate.

When a child is free to feel angry he will feel angry less often than otherwise.

As the child grows older he should be shown the difference between *feeling* anger and resentment, on the one hand, and the *physical expression* of these attitudes, on the other.

Our next point: parents should not oversell affection and its importance. A child should certainly be shown affection, but this should not be overdone. The overuse of giving and withholding affection as a means of controlling behavior is a mistake. It is of course one of the truisms of this society that affection and its "distribution" is a powerful motivating force for the control of behavior. Parents use the distribution of affection as a means of controlling their child from the moment he is born. When parents are being nice to the child and taking care of his needs, they tell the child they are full of love. If the child does anything bad they tell him they will not love him. In the families of most underachievers this is overdone. It would be far better for parents to matter-of-factly make a child desist from faulty actions without any reference to love or affection, implicitly as well as explicitly. When the child can understand words he can merely be told his faulty actions must be stopped because they are not in his own best interests. Many underachieving children come to feel the receiving of affection is "all important." It is because affection has been oversold that so many underachievers are pleasant to be with. Many of them have been made to feel the only safe emotion is affection. On the surface these underachievers are extremely pleasant. Inwardly they seethe with resentment.

Discipline

Some parents believe that to make a child behave they have to show they "really mean business." Some professional people endorse this view. "Show the child how angry you are," they say, "then he will listen." This is silly—and it wastes energy. The child should learn his parents are every bit as serious when speaking calmly as when they are screaming. It is far better that the child realize his parent intends to be obeyed, even in the absence of enraged anger.

A *consistent* program of discipline will help here. If you are a nervous and fussy parent and are forever annoyed by the child's actions and misactions, you *must* be inconsistent. Only a superman would be consistent about discipline if almost everything the child does calls for discipline. Parents should decide more or less in advance what should be disciplined, and stick to this decision—unless some serious modification is called for. They should make the list of don'ts a fair one—for the sake of their own sanity. Keep in mind that children pay more attention to nonverbal cues than to verbal ones. If a parent disciplines with an enraged look, a vocal tone five times higher than usual, and limbs trembling, the child will feel hated and unloved, no matter what he is told verbally. Discipline should be applied as matter-of-factly as possible, and should not be applied at all if the only "crime" has been an outburst of anger on the part of a young child. Actually the means of punishment (physical, withholding privileges, etc.) is secondary in importance to the emotional attitude that accompanies the discipline. If a child is about to hack away at a piece of furniture or a sibling and will not respond to a verbal request to cease and desist, he should be physically carried away from the scene of the "crime" with the matter-of-fact pronouncement: "You cannot do that." No invectives about parental love need be brought up.

Some parents (and some experts) say it is impossible and "not right" to punish children in a rather calm and matter-of-fact manner. But it is a myth that anger cannot be reasonably controlled, or that the regulating of anger will somehow "hurt" the parent and make him "neurotic" and "frustrated." Most anger has an irrational component. Most people become angry because they think they are being personally attacked. When the child acts "wrongly," most parents do not consider the wrong behavior an inefficient act to be corrected, but rather consider the wrong act a personal insult. They think to themselves: "What right has the child to do this to me! The ungrateful wretch!" And so they become angry. Or else the parent feels the child's act reflects poorly on his or her child rearing ability. This parent takes "wrong" behavior as a personal insult to his own capabilities, and responds with bitter resentment. And of course an inward fear of anger usually intensifies the anger. Some parents scream and yell at the child simply because they are lazy. Parents who would rather do this than rise from their chairs, pay a large price for such laziness.

Teaching the Child to Distinguish between Feelings and Actions

The system of rewards and punishments that parents, and later society, use to control individual behavior should not become overly linked with inner emotional feelings. A child may rightly learn, for example, "If I hit my little brother, my parents will punish me." But he should not come to believe: "If I feel angry at my little brother, my parents will hate me." An adult may come to know: "If I hit that policeman in the nose, I will be arrested." He should not come to know: "If I feel angry at that policeman for giving me a ticket, I will have committed a sin." We carry our feelings around with us and cannot escape from them. We should feel free to experience any feeling—and not have to worry about our sense of psychological security. The underachiever must be made to know he is free to *feel* any feeling at all, although he is not free to *act out* any feeling at all.

Some parents can inhibit angry feelings in their child by most subtle means. For example, grossly overaffectionate displays, activated the instant the child seems angry, is a very subtle and debilitating control maneuver on the part of many parents. The child is made to feel irritable and guilty whenever angry feelings arise within him.

25

The Development of
Self-Confidence

An Overview

Three conditions must be met if a child is to develop adequate self-confidence. First, it is important he have a relatively consistent self picture. Children who lack self-confidence in general, and underachievers in particular, had or have parents who make incompatible demands of them, demanding that the child be two or more different people at the same time. The child is usually commanded to be nonassertive and nonangry; at the same time he is pushed to be an assertive competitor. Along the same lines, the child should have reasonably realistic expectations for himself. If there is a great gap between what the child expects of himself and what he can reasonably do, self-confidence will suffer. A gap *will* exist if the parents make inconsistent and unrealistic demands of the child.

Second, sarcasm should be avoided as a disciplinary weapon.

Third, it is important that a child not link his entire sense of self worth with his ability to achieve. Here are some practical suggestions which will help the child develop self-confidence.

A Consistent Self Picture

A healthy self picture is reasonably free of internal contradictions. This does not mean the healthy person is rigid and unable to accept mixed feelings (consciously) about many things. The typical underachiever has been made to feel he must inhibit anger but at the same time be an aggressive and assertive competitor.

To be a human means to live with some contradictions, but this is a matter of degree. A person forced to harbor many mutually exclusive but equally compelling attitudes is doomed to a life of tension. He will be anxious because so many of the situations he runs into will evoke two or more mutually exclusive responses at one and the same time. For example, when the underachiever is challenged, part of his personality wants to respond in an assertively competitive manner. But because he so fears aggressively-tinged action tendencies, another part of his personality demands an anxious retreat. And both parts of his personality feel an "equal" compulsion to so act. The frustration that results from this psychological trap will cause even more aggressively-tinged anger, and the distress increases. The passive-aggressive orientation is an attempted compromise to this "impossible" situation. The organism reacts with anxiety to a situation where two or more "opposite" responses are being demanded at the same time. It is the organism's way of showing that something is wrong. Anxiety is the organism's way of showing it is receiving incompatible "orders" for action, *and there is no "safe" way to choose among these alternative courses of action.* The underachiever adopts a passive-aggressive orientation in a desire to reduce anxiety. It is his inefficient compromise to the fact that opposite demands are being made of him.

A good start would be for the parent to sit down and figure out what he wants of his child and what he expects in the area of general behavior. It may be found that two different reactions are being demanded of the child at the same time. The parents may like the child to be exhibitionistic in front of adult friends. But these same parents may object to exhibitionistic tendencies when alone with the child. Another thing: it is quite likely that at least one of the underachiever's parents "pushes" the child to defend his opinions and rights when with his friends. He may be denied these same rights at home. The child is "commanded" to be bright and creative in school, and yet it may annoy his parents if he clutters the house with his collections or other play materials. His parents may demand he be curious and exploratory in school, but yet have a rigid set of values to severely limit his freedom at home. These are just some of the glaring inconsistencies we have found in the families of underachievers (as well as with other neurotics).

More Remarks on Discipline

Parents can find out if inconsistent things are being demanded of the child by making a list of their own likes and dislikes. It is surprising that some of the behavior patterns liked in certain situations are violently disliked in other contexts. The child is cute if he talks back in one situation, but is berated violently for doing the exact same thing another time. Now it *is* true that certain reactions are indeed appropriate in some situations but not in others. And it is not inconsistent of parents to expect a certain type of reaction in one situation but not in others. Taking the shoes off and relaxing is appropriate behavior for some occasions, but not on others. However, two things should be kept in mind.

1. The idea of "proper" and "improper" should not extend to the domain of inner feelings. The child should never come to believe that a certain feeling is wrong or improper.

2. When a certain reaction is appropriate in one situation but not in another, the child should be so advised.

Most parents apply rules and discipline uncritically. They administer discipline when personally angry or annoyed, rather than when appropriate. Discipline is warranted when the child is doing something detrimental to his or other people's goals and aspirations or physical safety. *Actions* should be disciplined (not feelings) if they are potentially harmful to the child or to others. The purpose of discipline is to teach the child adaptive ways of living. It should not be administered out of personal malice, anger, or annoyance. Even though a parent may reasonably be annoyed or angered by certain actions of the child, this anger need not be played up nor carry over to the area of discipline.

Identifying Contradictory Parental Expectations

We believe parents of underachievers will find the following contradictions if they make a list of likes and dislikes:

"I like the child when he does things very well."

"I like the child when he stands up for his rights."

"I dislike seeing the child make stupid mistakes."

"I dislike the child when he is angry."

The contradictions are obvious. One cannot do things well without making mistakes. One cannot stand up for one's rights without sometimes harboring angry feelings.

Make your own list, and consider it at length.

Another Remark on the Self Picture

Although the child's own attitudes toward himself determine and make up his self picture and his sense of worth, these personal attitudes are probably carbon copies of his parents' attitudes. The best way to make sure the child will have positive attitudes toward himself is for the parents to have positive attitudes toward him. Much of what the child thinks about himself is what the parents think of him. If the parents "see" an inept, imperfect specimen, so does the child. On the other hand, healthy admiration and respect are "catching."

Sarcasm and Its Relation to Self-Confidence

One of the most brutal ways a parent can punish a child (it is usually done by the father) is by sarcasm—by mocking, sadistic criticism. If a parent should find himself belittling the child in this way, he should take a long and hard look at his purposes. A frustrated and inadequate parent is usually the type who will do this sort of thing. The father who does not think much of himself uses sarcasm on his child. This father is usually a petty person who wants to imagine that all of his offspring are "perfect." He wants them to be the lumps of perfection he secretly knows he isn't but wishes he were. He is offended by anything they do which he considers stupid. He is mocking and sarcastic whenever a mistake is made (unless he makes it). This orientation is a most negative one. If a father finds himself using sarcasm, he should most certainly ask himself why. First, he will find he is personally offended or insulted by the child's actions. He will find he is really less concerned with the actual effectiveness of his child's actions, and more concerned with the fact that these actions personally insult him. And if he searches long enough, he will finally find he secretly expects others to criticize *him* for any imagined shortcoming in the child—even if minor or petty. And if he has enough insight, he may further be able to discover he has an overly rigid set of personal standards to which he clings, irrationally identifying these standards with his own psychological well-being.

This father does not give his child a chance to live his own life. He is commanding the child to meet adult standards of perfection at a time when this is not only impossible but even undesirable. If a father finds he cannot stop himself from being sarcastic, he should seek professional aid. This parent may not have a serious problem, but it is one that is particularly debilitating to the child. It is more rare for a mother to be openly sarcastic, but not impossible. The same things we have been saying about fathers apply equally to mothers. Mothers cut their children down in other ways, usually by refusing them personal freedom and individual identities.

A Mirror to Hate

You have probably heard the term "projection" many times. One use of this term refers to those instances in which a person dislikes something about another person because he fears this thing is true of himself. Fathers who fear personal weakness in themselves cannot stand anything that resembles personal weakness in their children. Whenever the child shows signs of personality weakness, such a father becomes infuriated. He usually uses sarcasm to punish and hurt the child. One father who was notoriously unclean and unkempt yelled angrily at his child for these very same things. He constantly picked on his child because of the child's poor appearance. This father did not realize he dressed and groomed himself much the same way as his child. He was quite amazed when these conditions were pointed out to him.

Another father, let us say, cannot stand to see his child lose at anything, whether this be a sporting competition or a test in school. He resents the fact that his child appears to be weak. This scares him because he fears he himself may be weak. He sarcastically punishes his child whenever the child does not appear to be the zenith of male superstrength.

The Sense of Self Worth and the Fear of Failure

The parents of underachievers believe their *own* senses of self worth depend entirely on what they can do. Further, most parents of underachievers desire to "prove something" to their own parents. Many of them, especially mothers, want to show they are ideal parents. Irving Harris, in the book, *Emotional Blocks to Learning* (Free Press, 1961), found that most achieving children have achieving fathers. Thus it is apparently a "good" thing for a father to be an achiever. Our data support this finding. However it is one thing for a father to be an achiever and another thing for him to be a fussy perfectionist who insists on the absolute "ultimate" from the child. Parents of many underachievers resent their own parents. They often seek revenge, trying to show them up. One way they can do this is by having academically perfect children. And they end up with the very opposite of what they push for.

The first general recommendation: the child should be made to feel he is loved for himself and that any extra good feeling which comes his way as a reward for good work is quite secondary. To make the child feel this way, long-winded speeches in the face of opposite emotional attitudes are futile. Parents should treat school work with friendly interest. The parents, however, should not indicate that they think *everything* depends on the ability to accomplish. You will notice this is essentially a matter of degree. How, then, is a parent to know the right degree or mixture of these attitudes?

Along with the valuing of excellence, parents should seek out areas of interaction with their children other than those involving achievement or successful competition. Most parents find little enough to talk about with their children anyhow. They find they usually end up by speaking about school work or about how successful the child has been in conquering something. Other areas of interaction can involve television, movies, books, or almost anything. These discussions should be friendly and perhaps "intellectual," but should not involve the idea of "being better than someone else" as the main point. If the child develops a healthy intellect and an inquisitive mind, he will be appropriately competitive on his own.

It is important for each parent to spend some time with the child. The (emotional) *quality* of the time spent is more important than the *frequency* of the encounters. Many wives feel their husbands do not spend enough time with the children. But even if the father cannot spend much time with his child, he can at least be in a pleasant mood when he does. A father should be emotionally accessible to his child. If the child approaches the father while he is reading a newspaper, the father may react in anger and tell the child to go away. But he could also matter-of-factly say that when he is through with the newspaper he will be available.

Parents usually rationalize by telling themselves how competitive the job situation is today and how selective colleges are becoming. They try to tell themselves their demands for perfect work are in the child's best interests. They will tell themselves that good jobs are only given to the best students. And it is true colleges *are* becoming more selective, and it is true that the job situation is gradually changing so as to favor the person with the better education. But even though this is true, it does not negate what we have been saying. Colleges are becoming more selective and employees will be more carefully screened, but it is also true that constant demands for perfection will result in anything but good accomplishment. The parent can only know for sure how he stands on these matters after a soul-searching experience. If a parent does overvalue achievement, things must be changed so as to make the child realize that although excellent accomplishment is valued, he is not *commanded* to be perfect. The child must come to realize his parents do not intend to stop loving him if he is not a perfect accomplisher. Indeed, they should want to show him they are more interested in his enjoying the concrete work than in any other thing.

Developing Independence

Real psychological independence means that the child will accept the responsibility of evaluating his own actions. This is not easy for the underachiever. By his inept actions he blackmails his parents into treating him as a dependent child. He is not aware of this. Even nondemanding parents somehow end up with the job of nagging him to do his homework, prepare for exams, turn in assignments on time. The child balks. Unconsciously, he has planned the arrangement.

Self-responsibility is handed back to the child by using the nondirective approach formulated by psychologist Carl Rogers. Should the child shout, complain, whine, brag, provoke, challenge, attack, retreat, or refuse to work, the parents merely reflect back to the child his own words or feelings, *in an emotionally neutral way.*

"I won't do my homework!" shouts the child. The parents say: "You feel it is unfair of us to ask you to do your homework." Later, they may add: "You're upset because we tell you to do things you know you should do on your own." No matter the retort, the parents reflect it. If this is not done in an emotionally neutral way, or if the child feels manipulated, nothing will be accomplished. The approach will not work as a short-term expedient. Time is required; the philosophy behind it—giving the child the right of self-determination—must become a genuine part of the parental outlook.

Should the child slam a door in anger, the parents might simply say: "You're angry." If the action must be stopped, they add: "But you cannot do that." At first the child will walk off when his thoughts or actions have been reflected. Soon—not right away—the child will say to himself: "Gee, why *did* I do that?" Since he is not attacked either by word, tone, or gesture, he will eventually feel no need to break off the conversation, or refuse to realize what he is doing. Gradually, he will accept the responsibility for thinking about and evaluating what he is doing *on his own.* At this point the approach—which by now has become a guiding philosophy—will have achieved its purpose.

26.

The Urge to
Compete

The Fearful Father

Some fathers cannot tolerate competition from their children. The father who cannot tolerate a successful child does not, of course, realize this. On a conscious level he may think he wants a successful and victorious son. Unconsciously, however, he cannot tolerate having a son who is a "winner." He feels very insecure whenever he appears second best in the eyes in his wife. He desires exclusive possession of his wife. He is insecure and dependent, and hence counts on his wife to be like a mother to him. He may have had a father who made him dependent and unsure of his own abilities. Now *he* does not want to have a competitor who can do things successfully. He is afraid his wife will be taken from him, and will no longer be his exclusive pillar of support. He usually belittles his child and uses sarcasm as a means of punishment. He is fearful his male child will replace him. Quite commonly his own father had similar fears and fought him for exclusive possession of his mother.

Another reason the father cannot tolerate a victorious son is that he feels inadequate as a male. He is never sure of himself. His own father probably treated him the same way he now treats his son. He may have had successful older siblings with whom he feared to compete. Now that he is grown up he passes on these neurotic fears to his child.

There is one other common condition which may cause the child to inhibit competitive attitudes—a father who is very weak or who is absent from the home. A father who has a very weak personality is looked upon with mixed emotions by the boy child. This child does not like the weakness he sees in his father. He wishes his father were stronger so as to offer boundless protection. At the same time, he has a desire to outdo him. If the father is so weak that he presents no challenge or no inhibiting force to the child, the child will feel he is winning over an opponent about whom he has very mixed feelings (love, fear, contempt, etc.). The child will equate "winning out" with aggressiveness, and will suffer guilty feelings. These same processes may take place if the father is absent a good deal of time. The child begins to feel he has exclusive ownership of mother. Deep down inside he realizes, however, his father would hate this, and is hence a potential enemy who desires to punish him. When father is absent, there is no effective inhibiting force against the child's naturally possessive attitude toward mother. A forbidden object is being made "too available." As he comes to feel his mother is his exclusive property, he simultaneously feels he is taking something that does not belong to him. A fear of retaliation may develop. These forces should be balanced. A father who so fears "losing" his wife may constantly "down" his son and thereby rob the son of confidence. This is intensified if the mother is overly close to the child. The problem is successfully handled by the secure father, with whom the child can identify. If the father is adequately secure, no special attention need be given to these processes, which resolve themselves naturally under positive conditions.

And so here is another reason why a child may fear to be competitively victorious. He fears he is taking something away from a person toward whom he has very mixed feelings. He both loves and hates, admires and fears, a person he does not know whether to imitate or "steal" from.

Fathers and Sons

It is important a father clarify his innermost attitudes toward his son. He may ask himself the following questions:

"When I am in an argument with the boy, do I yell at him if he seems to be making better points than I?"

"Will I allow him to have opinions, especially if they are better opinions than my own?"

"When he is asking intelligent questions, do I make fun of him and pretend the questions are not intelligent?"

"Do I have to get in the last word when there is a discussion?"

"Do I belittle him after he has done something well, rationalizing to myself I don't want him to get a swelled head?"

This next one is especially important and often difficult to observe:

"Do I become irritable when the child is acting intelligently?"

This last point deserves careful attention. Many a father finds himself becoming irritable when his child is acting in an assertive and intelligent manner. This father often does not realize just what it is that is putting him on edge, but his irritability is clear.

27

The Perfectionistic Child

Some children are fussy about everything they do. They are meticulous about their homework and about rules of games in which they participate. In other words, they are as fussy about random play activity as they are about structured work tasks. This degree of fussiness, carried as it is to extremes, is a negative attribute. This child works under a strain. He usually tries to dominate games in which he plays. He wants everything done his way. He infuriates his friends because they know he bosses them from insecurity rather than genuine strength. Children can tell the difference between a leader who leads on the basis of natural ability and one who pushes others around because of nervousness and insecurity. This insecure child typically speaks in a high-pitched, rather nervous voice, and often suffers from disturbing nightmares. He may have phobias—intensely fearing certain things or situations. He usually has superior intelligence.

This child has a severe and restrictive conscience. He is his own worst enemy. He usually demands perfection and will settle for nothing less. He cannot stand inconsistency, either in himself or in his environment, and hence tries to control everything and every person with whom he comes in contact. He wants to make sure he will not run into any inconsistency. He tries to gear things so that he can tell in advance how they will turn out. He must have certain things go as he foresees them. It would be anxiety-arousing for this child to encounter unexpected events. He often appears to be selfish. He must set things up so as not to encounter anything not planned for. In trying to meet these demands, he must order others about.

When underachievement is associated with this type of problem, here is what should be done:

1. This child must be made more comfortable with his own feelings, especially with the feeling of anger. This is a child who greatly fears his own aggressive attitudes, much more so than does the typical underachiever. It is of prime importance to carry out the recommendations specified in Chapter 24. The idea is to make the child feel more comfortable with his anger, but still feel he has the guidance and support of a trusted adult. The fussy child is often that particular passive-aggressive child who has occasional outbursts of anger. He can be nasty and annoying, makes many demands on people, but cannot really help it. It should not be held against him (as the parents of this child are likely to do).

2. The fussy child must be taught to be flexible in his standards. He should be shown that subjective standards may vary according to subjective purposes. He need not apply the same rigid rules of perfection to play activities. The child should be taught to evaluate different facets of his own performance according to his different purposes. The perfectionistic child generally treats everything in his environment alike. He is always in one mood—perfectionistic—no matter the situation. To him, play activity is every bit as important and compelling as school activity. Now it is quite true that children assign more importance to play activity than do adults, and are serious about their play. Neverthe-

less, this is carried to extremes with the fussy child. He must be taught to allow his standards to vary in accordance with the importance of the different tasks in which he is interested.

3. It is very important to stay relaxed in the presence of the perfectionistic child. Fussy children do so many annoying things that this is not easy. If discipline is called for, it must be carried out in as relaxed a manner as is humanly possible. The fussy child reacts in a negative way to anxiety in his environment. Anxiety in the parents tends to ruffle his entire sense of self-confidence to an untoward degree.

4. It is important to encourage the perfectionistic child to be "realistic." He already suffers from an abundance of fantasy. Indeed, he should be made to feel comfortable with his fantasies, and *should not be* discouraged from having them. However, he *should be* actively encouraged to size things up accurately. If he has faulty opinions, these should be brought to his attention in a relaxed and spontaneous manner. The perfectionistic child may think that others are more angry at him than they really are. The fussy child is a great one for misunderstanding other people. If he assumes that another child is angry at him, the matter should be investigated and the truth brought to light. The perfectionistic child has a tendency to indulge in "magical thinking." He develops many ideas about the world which are untrue, and he suffers from many illusions. He often harbors the idea that witches and monsters are real. No matter how he rationally tells himself they do not exist, a substantial part of his personality clings to the idea, and the child suffers accordingly. Hence his misinterpretations and misunderstandings should be brought to light and gently discussed. It is important to do this in a very relaxed manner. The perfectionistic child already suffers from an overabundance of anxiety-arousing fantasy. If the parents become anxious over his fantasies, misunderstandings, and misbeliefs, they will communicate this anxiety to him. If he is made anxious over his fantasies, more harm will have been done than good. If they begin to make him too nervous, he will be nervous almost all of the time, simply because his mind is so often preoccupied with fantasy productions.

5. If the fussy and meticulous child described in this chapter stays "fussy" for any prolonged length of time, professional counsel is strongly advised. The chances are that he is developing an obsessional neurosis, which is best treated in its early stages.

28.

The Child with
Inner Doubts

Many psychological and constitutional factors are at work in producing a child who has an obsessional orientation. We often find the mother or father (usually the father) puts too much emphasis on rigid perfectionism. A stuffy and pedantic father does a lot of harm to his children. It is true that fussy people can be efficient in some things, but they are efficient at a disadvantage. Overly perfectionistic parents should heed this last sentence. You may be a fussy, perfectionistic parent and your child may still be an achiever; but this largely in spite of your efforts, not because of them.

Fussy and perfectionistic children are usually capable of good work only up to a point. If this crucial point is surpassed the child usually falls apart and the quality of his work drops.

Many perfectionistic parents try to impose their own standards on their children. However, it is one thing for an adult to be perfectionistic, and another thing for a child to have this orientation pushed on him. When a child is ordered to be perfectionistic, it can only retard self-confidence and the pursuit of excellence. The art of being an efficient human should develop gradually. It cannot be implanted "full-grown."

The father of the obsessional child is often sarcastic, bright, and achievement-oriented. The idea of "intellectual superiority" is important to him. He often makes his male children feel intellectually puny. He makes his child feel that only superior work is allowed (while maintaining sole right to define "superiority"). On the surface the child becomes docile and submissive. The importance of being liked by males, particularly older males in positions of authority, becomes exaggerated in his mind. Much fantasy and worry is spent in thinking of ways to please male authority figures and of ways to avoid unpleasantness with them. In more extreme cases the child develops a passive and submissive streak in his personality. But that is only half of the story. For this child is basically stubborn. He likes to be victorious. Part of his personality has been taught that perfection and "victory" are important. And consequently that part of his personality that feels safe only under conditions of victory comes into conflict with that part of his personality that wants to be submissive to males, to win and maintain love and "safety." This is one of the basic dilemmas of the child with the obsessional orientation. They are being ordered to be submissive and docile to win and maintain paternal support; at the same time they are being ordered to be intelligently victorious. The two orders are incompatible.

The fathers of such children should keep the following in mind.

1. A perfectionistic outlook cannot be imposed on someone else. A desire to do excellent work must come gradually.

2. The father of the obsessionally-oriented child should devote some time to thinking over the types of behavior he is demanding of the child. Does the child feel he must win love at all costs? Does the father make the child feel like a fool when something is done incorrectly? Is the child teased a good bit of the time? Is ridicule and punishment followed by displays of affection on the part of the father? Does the father demand final answers on all issues?

3. Of particular importance is how the father feels about the son-mother relation. Does the father become annoyed when the boy spends too much time with his mother? Does he secretly want the child to feel like an outsider in the family?

4. The father must carefully consider the nature of his relation with his child. Is the father unconsciously making the son feel puny, especially intellectually? Does the father implicitly "tell" his child that he, the child, is no match for him (the father)?

If "yes" is the answer to most of these questions, the child is probably overly perfectionistic, inclined to worry, and rapidly developing an obsessional orientation, if not a full-blown obsessional neurosis. If a steady program of applied "will power" cannot change things, this father is probably living an uncomfortable existence himself and would profit from a chance to talk things over with a professionally trained person.

29.

The Babyish Child

The idea of being a "baby" suggests itself to the underachiever as a solution to his problems. If he is a baby he will be loved, no matter what his achievements happen to be. And so the underachiever comes to find himself acting and thinking like a baby whenever he is under any stress. The likelihood of this solution being adopted by the underachiever is raised because of the natural tendency all people have to fall back to infantile ways of handling things when stress becomes unbearable. The human organism apparently fails to consider the pertinence, relevance, or effectiveness of these infantile maneuvers when stress is intense. All organisms, by the way, not only human beings, seem to share this same tendency. The underachiever desperately wants to be loved, but he fears he cannot meet the necessary conditions (perfect achievement).

To guard against babyish behavior, parents must make the

child realize he is and will be loved without fulfilling special conditions, or, more practically, *that the conditions are minimal.* A reasonable "return" is expected of the child by the parents. The child is expected to conform to certain rules and regulations of the home. And he is expected to meet *certain* wishes and demands of his parents. However, the child should not come to feel he must never feel angry in order to receive love and affection from his parents, and he should never come to feel that absolutely perfect accomplishment is demanded of him.

Children who show a pronounced tendency to regress usually like to maintain skills that once impressed their parents. The regressive child is much more concerned than most other children with impressing and pleasing his or her parents. And so the regressive child will often become adept at reading aloud. This is usually an unfortunate thing. For the child comes to pay so much attention to his outward performance (pronouncing words) that he comes to forget the main purpose of reading, which is the gathering of information and experience. He ignores the actual meaning of the material he is supposedly reading. He reads out loud with apparent feeling and understanding. However, it often becomes obvious later that he has little idea of what he reads. He may have been encouraged when young to stand in front of groups and read out loud in a singsong voice. The parents and the guests made a fuss over his magnificent reading ability. The child comes to sacrifice the meaning of the material for a good show. His parents are surprised to find out later he has a reading problem. Because they are so impressed by this oral recitation, the child ignores the main purpose of reading—communication.

The child should not be encouraged to be overly impressed with essentially childish displays of "talent," especially reading aloud. Reading should definitely be encouraged, but emphasis should be placed on the meaning and implications of the material rather than on the oral show.

30.

Trapped by Words: The Fear of Being Ordinary

Most underachieving children have a fear of being ordinary. Their parents have made them feel exceptional things are expected of them. They come to think that if they are not exceptional they are total failures. Two negative things follow. For one thing, we have shown the peculiar way in which this desire actually *prolongs* the educatonal problem. He cannot be extraordinary by virtue of excellent grades, but he can be by virtue of poor grades! Part of his personality is fooled into thinking it is "good" to have an educational problem. Parents can help the child overcome this strange desire by helping him to develop some other area of special competence or distinction while playing down the notion that self worth is *entirely* dependent on special competence. It is helpful, however, for the child to feel important in at least one area. This area should be something at least partially intellectual, like arts and crafts, model building, etc. The child's pride needs a lift. He wants to feel out-of-the-ordinary in at least one area. Helping him gain distinction in some area is a rational approach to the problem. It would be the job of the psychotherapist to handle the *irrational* way the child has been meeting this demand for distinction (by clinging to poor work). The parents have two jobs. One is to help the child realize that although it may be meritorious to strive for distinction, the intensity of this desire should be appropriate and rational. Secondly, it is up to the parents to help the child feel competent in at least one area. The underachiever gets a terrific boost out of being competent, even if the competence extends to but a single area. Good functioning in one area is a first positive step for the underachiever.

The debilitating thing about a desire to be nonordinary is that the neurotic person rarely defines for himself just what he should do to be distinctive Here we deal with a general neurotic phenomenon. Like all other neurotics, underachievers are unable to accept the idea of "degree." To himself a neurotic underachiever is either a "success" or a "failure." And yet what is a success? When is one no longer a failure? These are difficult questions for all of us, but particularly the underachievers. It is particularly damaging from a psychological standpoint when a person does not accept the idea of *degrees of success*. Here is a crucial point. *The underachiever, like most neurotics, cannot stand the prospect of improvement by degrees.* He wants to start out at the "end." He wants to be there before he starts. This makes the treatment of an underachiever difficult. His grades will not change overnight but only gradually. And the underachiever wants perfection at the outset. He is frightened that he may study and study and only improve a little or not at all. This is still too terrifying to his shaky self-confidence. The underachiever cannot tolerate the idea of gradual success.

The only way parents can help out in this area is by giving the child some knowledge of the shackling power of words. The child should be told it is senseless to apply damaging labels to himself. He should be encouraged to view and judge his own life in terms of degrees, and not in terms of absolute end-points. The parents might read some books on general semantics (such as have been written by Stuart Chase and Wendell Smith).

31.

For the Overprotective Mother

Life itself is a prison for the overprotective mother; it is seen as a program of things that must be done rather than as a process which unfolds. When she wakes up in the morning, she has a mental list of things which she feels must be done. She lacks a feeling of inner freedom, and rarely feels "free" to enjoy life. She feels frustrated almost all of the time, and why not? Anyone would be staggered by the load this woman irrationally assumes she must carry. It is often said that the overprotective mother really resents responsibility. However, this is only partially true, and even then it is true only in a special sense. These women have the feeling they must live up to unrealistic standards, just as they are making their own children live up to unrealistic standards. They resent responsibility not because there is something inherently displeasing about responsibility, but rather because they irrationally assume they have "total responsibility." This mother not only feels responsible for the mechanical workings of the home, but even for the varying moods of the people in it. If the child has a gloomy mood, she feels responsible.

When one works with the overprotective mother in psychotherapy, one fact stands out: the mother has a good number of inhibited angers and resentments. Many feel their own parents were perfectionists. They feel the same thing is desired and expected of them. They all seem to have the conviction that their children are test cases by means of which they are personally evaluated.

The "overprotective" orientation is difficult to change, and generally requires professional handling. A nervous and overinvolved parent cannot simply switch to another personality at will. However, we advise the use of reflective and critical insight at this point. The overprotective mother is usually recalcitrant about seeking professional help on her own. She rationalizes this in a typical way: she tells herself it would be wrong to spend her family money on herself. With her typical "martyr" method, she explains away her position. Every mother should consider if she meets the above mentioned criteria of the overprotective mother. If so, she should seek professional counsel.

32

The Eternal Triangle and
the Fear of Success

The Oedipal situation in the case of the young boy refers to the fact that he will see his father as a rival in a battle for mother's exclusive love. One aspect of the Oedipal situation is the jealousy that exists between a father and his son. Psychoanalysts feel the son and father are enmeshed in a serious and earnest conflict for the exclusive love of the mother.

Whether or not this is true—most evidence indicates it is—we do know that many fathers are overly jealous of their children, particularly their male children. Such a father is typically sarcastic and rejecting toward his male children, particularly his first born. He lets his child know he will love him only if he is no threat. The child sees that efficient behavior threatens his father.

When a father is jealous of his son, a keen tension comes to exist between them. The father for his part does everything he

146

can to discourage the son from doing anything too well. Consciously, he may not realize this, but in many subtle and devious ways he is undermining the child's confidence.

Another thing which contributes, or may contribute, to the child's fear of success is a weak or absent father. If a father has a weak personality or is absent from the home a good deal of the time, the child will begin to imagine that mother is too much his exclusive property. Yet, underneath, he realizes that father would violently dislike such a thing. The child feels guilty as though he were taking exclusive possession of a person who should be shared. If he senses an underlying weakness in his father's personality, this guilt may be especially strong. He not only fears taking advantage of a potential enemy, but feels that a source of support is letting him down. This guilt may give him a fear of success, such as we here describe. (In addition, an absent-father situation can cause many inconsistencies in the child's sense of sexual identity. This matter would have to be clarified by the professionally trained therapist.) When the child feels guilty because of a weak father, he may decrease his own effectiveness, hoping thereby to get rid of his guilt feelings, but also hoping to "boost" his father to a more "godlike" position.

If the child sees his mother dominating his father, this will contribute to the above conflict. A wife who "takes over" the masculine role in the family makes the father appear weak. This may increase the child's guilt. All of this is further complicated by the fact that a weak father provides no adequate object with which the son can identify. A male child best develops a consistent sense of male identity when he has an adequate male figure whom he can imitate.

A father must think over what role or roles he really plays in his family. He should seek advice from his wife on this so as to get an outside (but possibly biased) opinion. A husband who is dominated by his wife should talk the situation over with her. Professional help is usually advisable in such conditions. A father should ask himself how his son or children see him. If he is weak, absent, or dominated by his wife, he would do well to ask himself

why this is the case. Was his own father passive? Is he too insecure about his wife's love? Is his wife running the entire family?
Just how jealous is he of his son?

33.

Defiant Parents

Fathers who harbor resentment of authority had, in all likelihood, fathers who would not tolerate the expression of anger. From this began a passive-aggressive streak in the future father of the underachiever. These fathers are afraid to express their resentments openly. This is par for the course with the passive-aggressive individual. However, with some fathers the resentment of authority becomes an all-consuming motive. He may decide to battle the school his child attends. Unconsciously he is also making sure his son will remain a failure and hence non-competitive with him, the father.

Consequently, he refuses to believe his son has an educational problem; something must instead be wrong with the school or with the teacher. He communicates this idea to the child. The child, of course, is quite willing to blame things on the school. He would like nothing better than to let himself off the hook for his poor work. This father reinforces his child's search for a non-efficient escape hatch. They side up together against the school. Long-drawn-out senseless arguments begin between the parent and the school. Since the school's staff feels attacked, a counter-attack is launched. Someone in the school system is offended by the parent and the battle is on. The child is forgotten. The parent wants to win; the school people want to win.

Shep was a boy of fifteen. His school work had been rather poor in the eighth and ninth grades. Shep had the personality of a typical underachiever. He feared failure. He became defiant. He adopted a tough-guy attitude. He was nasty to his teachers. He played the role of "bad-man." He was not completely aware of his behavior. He provoked his teachers, and when they became annoyed with him, he explained his poor work on the basis of their dislike. "How can I do good work?" he would ask. "My teachers have it in for me." Shep let himself off the hook by telling himself he did poor work because his teachers hated him. They really did not like him. But he had set the stage to force them to dislike him. They found him a pugnacious and irritating child. But the point is that Shep himself made things this way. Shep's father *and* mother reinforced his stand. Since both of them resented authority, they assumed the school was to blame, and lost little time in becoming enmeshed in a bitter battle. The situation ended up in our office a number of months later. Shep's parents had to be shown what they were doing. They were using Shep to live out their own neurotic motives. Shep and his parents are currently receiving psychotherapy. In addition, Shep is being tutored in some school subjects. Since the treatment program has just started, no final word can be given on this case.

Parents who tend to side with their children against the school should seriously consider why they do so. Each parent may ask:

"Why am I really battling the school?"

"Do I resent the fact they are trying to *blame me?*"

"Do I think 'Who do *they* think they are, giving us this trouble?'"

"What are my general attitudes toward authority?"

"What is positively accomplished by arguing with the school?"

34.

Parents Who Fight

Some think parents should indeed argue in front of their children. "Why not? Let the children learn this is the way of life," argue the advocates of this position. Another school argues a child derives his sense of security and well-being through the stability of his parents individually and through the stability of their relationship. This side claims that arguments between parents shake the child's sense of security at a basic and deep-seated level.

As usual, stock rules and "sides" are generally exaggerated. Whether or not parents should argue in front of children depends on several things: the nature of the argument (if it involves the child it should *not* be in front of him), the manner in which the parents argue (if they shout, curse, and call each other names, the child should definitely not be present), and the frequency and intensity with which these arguments occur. The chances are that if the arguments are frequent and violent, other things as well are wrong with the marriage (besides the arguments themselves). Frequent and intense arguments are bound to affect the child in a negative way. Parents should ask themselves the following questions to find out if they have a serious or a mild conflict between them. (These principles emerged from a study on marital compatibility done by B. B. and Dr. Sophie Gottlieb: The prediction of some aspects of marital compatibility by means of the Rorshach test. *Psychiatric Quarterly*, 1961, 35, Pages 281-303.

1. After the parents argue, do they talk things over in a more relaxed manner? And if they do, does this lead to a decrease in friction or to an increase in friction? If the parents are unable to talk things over in a more relaxed manner, once the heat of the battle has cooled, their incompatibility is more pronounced than if the opposite were true. And if talking things over leads to more rather than less friction, their incompatibility tends toward the more serious side.

2. Are the arguments over real and concrete issues, or does the least little thing start an argument? If a minor and trivial thing starts an argument, and this is a chronic state of affairs, then each argument is only a reflection of a more basic and deep-seated underlying friction. If the parents get the feeling that each argument is only a convenient battleground behind which lurks a long-standing war, the incompatibility is serious.

3. Are there differences in quality or only in frequency? By this is meant: Is there really a true qualitative difference between the aims, aspirations, feelings, and attitudes of each marriage partner? Or does each desire the same things but in differing amounts? For example, suppose both enjoy a night out. Suppose, however, that the wife would like more outings than the husband. In this instance there is no *qualitative* difference—both enjoy outings. There *is* a difference in frequency, however. This is not a serious threat to compatibility. Differences in frequency are not quite so important as are differences in quality. Suppose one enjoys going out, but the other *never* wants to go out. This would be a qualitative difference and would be more serious.

This same scheme can be applied to other areas: exchanges of affection, sexual intercourse, etc. The parents should decide if their differences are in quality or in frequency.

If the parents decide they have a seriously incompatible marriage, it would be wise for them to consult an individual trained to deal with such problems. More and more research is accumulating on marital compatibility, and the professionally trained person will have much to offer the stressful marriage.

Aside from this, there are only a few simple rules which should be followed as far as the child is concerned.

We feel there is little point in parents arguing in front of a child. There is nothing wrong with showing children that adults may argue but still love each other. However, it is a mistake to think that the child will draw this conclusion when the arguments are violent. He will detect the hate being cast back and forth.

The next important point is this. Two mates who argue should be careful not to use their child as a pawn in this battle. Among the more obvious things a parent may do is to embitter the child against the mate. One mate tries to gain the child's ear to the detriment of the other. A mother might try to convince the child how bad the husband is and how bad all men are, giving the child a distorted view of the world. This will be especially serious if the child in question happens to be a girl. The girl will form the opinion that all men are no good. Likewise, the father may try to gain the child's ear in order to downgrade the mother. This will not only shake the child's self-confidence, and give him or her a poor conception of the mother, but will also give a distorted view of females in general. Another obvious way a child may be harmed is if one or both of the parents take out their wrath against each other on the child. Suppose the parents become so angry at each other that they cannot find words to express their disgust. They may take out some of these angry feelings on the child. Especially damaging is the husband who complains the marital stress began with the birth of the child. This is frequently done.

Other more subtle things may happen when there is a deep hostility between the mates. Sometimes the mother will use the boy child as an emotional substitute for her husband. This mother lavishes all her affection and care on the child and expects him to be a junior husband.

Psychologists are often asked whether it is better for the children if two battling parents divorce, on the one hand, or continue to live together in spite of the disharmony, on the other. The answer depends on the individuals involved. If one of the battling parents is basically healthy from an emotional standpoint, and can regain his perhaps temporarily lost health by virtue of a divorce, the child would be better off with this healthy parent. On the other hand, a parent may be so dependent as to rule out the possibility of even a minimally satisfactory independent adjustment. Parents hung up or suspended by this issue should seek professional help.

35.

Some Principles of Studying

The typical underachiever has heard many lectures on study methods. But the child who is inwardly thwarted by emotional conflict cannot even learn proper study habits, just as he cannot absorb other material taught him. Other changes must be induced before or along with the teaching of proper study methods.

When we talk about "study principles" we talk of two areas. One area is concerned with motivational and readiness factors. Motivational factors have to do with the child's interest and desire to learn. If he lacks this interest, his teacher works at a disadvantage. "Readiness" refers to the child's developing a set of basic skills which will help him to learn.

The other area concerns the study methods themselves, such as the technique of taking notes, the technique of using inner self quizzes, etc.

Motivating and Preparing the Child

There are a number of ways to induce motivation or learning interest in a child. We have already mentioned the best way, i.e., for the parents to value education and the active pursuit of educational excellence around the home without ordering the child to do the same. It is far better for a child to think something is his own idea and that he is not acting on the push of an outside force. We believe the single best way to motivate a child to learn is to have him love, admire, and identify with a person who values education. This adult or parent "ideal" must be one who can tolerate intellectual competition from a child without conflict.

There are other ways to develop learning interest in a child. The child can be encouraged to think in terms of the origin of things, and to read books explaining why and how things work. On the other hand, he should be taught to appreciate beauty and skill for their own sake. The child should be taken on trips and exposed to a wide variety of experiences. It helps a great deal for the parents to have a good library containing many illustrated books. The parents should spend pleasant and relaxed hours looking over the books with the child.

Readiness refers to the cultivation of skills which will make learning more efficient, easy, and pleasant. Great care should be taken when the child is young in the way words are pronounced. It would be a decided disadvantage if the child develops what is termed an "auditory discrimination" problem (an inability to discriminate similar sounding speech units, like the *t* sound from the *d* sound, and so forth). While still young he should be encouraged to understand the left to right progression in reading. He should be encouraged to look at pictures critically, and to notice differences in visual shapes and configurations.

Some of these procedures are designed to develop interest in the child, and others to prepare him for the learning experience.

Methods of Learning

When confronted with a new subject the child should first try to bring to mind a well-ordered summary of what he already knows on this same topic. He should mobilize and pattern his knowledge on the particular subject. It is difficult to remember isolated bits of information. One should connect a new fact to organized facts already known on the same topic. Ideas cannot be efficiently recalled unless they are organized. Learning to relate new information to old information ordered in meaningful patterns is one of the most important study habit methods. Only when the child can thus connect a new bit of information to a meaningful structure of knowledge, consisting of patterned facts already known, will he truly "learn" the thing in question. This lineup and connection must be done a certain way, that is, verbalized in a coherent and structured manner. The child should not merely "scan" his ideas on the pertinent topic. He must act inwardly as though he were actually going to write a summary of his knowledge. Only in this way will the child know if he really understands the topic. *He must line up definite and finished sentences in his mind,* in summary fashion. Then he must fit the new information into this scheme. When he does this, he will truly understand and remember the new information. This method goes hand in hand with another method which should be used at the same time. When a child is about to study something, he should prepare himself for what he is about to learn. For example, suppose a child is going to study about Christopher Columbus. He could say something like the following to himself: "Now I am to study about an explorer. Explorers search for and discover new places or go to investigate faraway lands. What I am going to learn now is going to be about an explorer's life and the things that happened to him and how he influenced others." In a sense, he is preparing a "receptacle" in which to put his new learning. He is lining up categories into which he can put the new facts he is to be given.

Another very important study technique is self quizzing. It is well known that a person does not learn anything unless he can explain it to himself in his own words. A child must frequently pause in his learning process and tell himself what he has learned. A child must rephrase material in his own words to really learn it. Only in this way will the new information actually become a part of him and thus remain with him. The self quiz is a most important study method. A person must review what he is learning, and he must do this reviewing in his own words. If he only parrots what he has heard the new information will be stored as a short-lived message on a tape recorder. The tape will be too easily erased or the message "stored" in a nonrecoverable manner. More important than the actual questions he asks himself is the fact that the child is adopting an *active* approach to the learning task. Parents need not be initially concerned so much about the quality of the questions the child poses to himself, but rather about whether he indeed poses *any* questions. Naturally the brighter and more efficient children will pose the brighter questions, but the success of this technique is more due to the active orientation assumed than the quality of the questions posed.

Naturally, the quality of the achievement (excellent, mediocre, etc.) of which the child becomes capable will depend a great deal on the quality of the questions posed. If the questions posed are poor in quality because of conflicted attitudes, e.g. inhibited attention span, chronic doubts, desire to fail, need to cling to tiny isolated details, etc., the suggestions offered in the book should improve the situation. But the step between not asking any questions at all and asking some (any) questions is a much greater and more effortful step for the underachiever to take than that required to change poor into good grades.

We stress these psychological preparations because they are most frequently overlooked in books on study habits. These psychological preparations are more important in the learning process than the number of minutes devoted to studying or the particular way one chooses to make notations.

It is important that a child feel free to ask questions when he does not understand something. The one way to insure that your child will feel free to ask questions in school is to make him feel free to ask questions at home. If a child has been made to feel embarrassed or stupid when he asks something at home, he will be inhibited in his ability to ask questions in general. He will feel he should have understood things the first time around. This is important. For even very intelligent children cannot understand everything on the first hearing. Each person tends to learn or remember things in different ways. What makes sense to one person when spoken about one way, will make sense to another person only when spoken about in a different way. People learn and remember best when they can understand things in a way in keeping with what they already know. For this reason, a good teacher will strive to present new material in as many ways as possible. The teacher will have to be somewhat repetitive in that he or she must present new facts in many different ways so that what is being taught can "click" in as many minds as possible.

We have not mentioned those points which are covered in typical study habit books, which interested parents can consult. The type of desk used, the exact time when the homework is done, the exact amount of time spent on homework, the way notes are taken—all are of varying importance. They may be more important in a given case and less important in another; the things we have mentioned cover the heart of the active learning process.

36.

A Note to the Professional on
the Underachieving Child

Most underachieving children are pleasant to be with in spite of their passive-aggressive personalities. Many of them feel affectionate behavior is the only behavior permissible. In fact this is one of the reasons why they are so anxious in the face of angry feelings, and subsequently in the expression of any genuine emotional feelings. The underachiever, like anyone else, indeed feels angry on many occasions, but the ensuing anxiety and guilt rob him of self-confidence, and in addition his deep-seated inhibitions make him angry a good deal of the time. He is usually fun to be with, and often has a superior sense of humor. This outer façade of pleasantness does not depend upon the socio-economic level of the child. That is, the underachieving child from both lower and upper socio-economic levels is usually pleasant. (We do not refer to sociologically induced cases.) The underachiever is nonetheless quite difficult to approach psychotherapeutically. The passive-aggressive child shows up for each session in a seemingly affable and cooperative mood. But he does not actually enter wholeheartedly into the treatment program. For one thing, his resistant behavior is representative of his major method of handling difficulties—the passive-aggressive method. He cooperates on the surface, but actually will not talk about pertinent subjects, will usually not cooperate in reporting dreams (he claims he cannot remember them), or if he does report them, he reports so many of them as to become lost in a mass of unessential details. And he does these things with greater frequency and with greater tenacity than the usual neurotic. What is particularly disarming is the discrepancy between the outer condition (pleasantness) and the unconscious attitude (bitter rage).

The child has a hard time relating his emotional states to his school work. Most children fail to see the connection between their deep-seated feelings and the quality of their school work. They cannot see how their feelings toward their parents, for instance, can have anything to do with the quality of the work they do in school. This inability to see the connection between emotional states and school work presents a particular difficulty at the beginning in working with the underachiever. And even after much time has been spent in drawing the underachiever's attention to this relationship, it takes an awfully long time for the underachiever to really understand or to accept this relationship.

It is often a time-consuming process to bring the underachiever's work to an acceptable level. Although there are exceptions, most therapists agree that the process usually requires a minimum of one year. The longer a problem of underachievement has gone unattended, the longer is the treatment time required to effect any worthwhile change for the better. Poor work in the early grades robs a child of his foundation skills—skills by means of which he is to acquire the rest of his education. Parenthetically, we wish to add that schools should use their very best teachers in the first and second grades—the foundation years. The better pay and life of the secondary schoolteacher work against this ideal.

We have already mentioned some of the reasons why psychological treatment is such a time-consuming process with the underachiever. The passive-aggressive orientation usually becomes well entrenched in the personality structure of the child or adult who possesses it. The passive-aggressive person usually has little insight into his real inner attitudes. Because of the very nature of his major system of defense, passive aggressiveness, he is actually fighting the treatment process, albeit in his usual disguised and secretive passive manner. For another thing, the passive-aggressive person is actually afraid to express or even to experience any real and genuine emotion. Consequently, he has an intense fear of any type of emotional upheaval in his feelings. He will therefore resist a process which he believes may cause such a reaction.

A Psychotherapeutic Approach to Underachievement

A highly concrete psychotherapeutic approach is optimal in dealing with the underachiever, no matter the age of the particular child involved. We find it desirable to draw the child's attention to the very words he says to himself in general as he enters a class, and especially before taking a test. We aim to show the child how he is robbing himself of self-confidence by having a prior expectation of doing poorly. We point out in what ways the child is telling himself how horrible it would be to fail, and how he thinks it would be better not to try at all. Once we teach the child to "focus in" on the manner in which he is robbing himself of self-confidence, we begin a (loosely structured) review of the points covered in this work. The directiveness of the approach varies from case to case and is of course varied to fit the individual child. With some children, a very directive approach is warranted. Others make better progress with a more loosely structured program. We are never manipulative in the sense of "ordering" the child to adopt a point of view, or tricking him into admitting something about himself. Keep in mind that "directive approach" refers to the definite focus which is maintained, and not to our assuming a role of "teacher," "parent," or "prophet." In general, we follow this procedure:

1. The parents are seen. A program is instituted to remove underachievement-engendering patterns from the home. They are forewarned that the therapeutic procedure is time consuming and that they should not look for immediate improvements. If they are forever "looking over the shoulder" of the therapist, everybody, the child most of all, works at a disadvantage. If parents expect a smoothly rising curve of improvement, they will be disappointed and angered when they see that such improvement is not forthcoming. Everything is done to impress upon the parents a realization of the long term nature of the project. On the other hand, everything possible is done to alleviate the child's guilt that he is to blame for the time and expense of the therapeutic program. Parents are never allowed to send money in with the child. They are instructed not to talk about the time or the money involved in the program.

2. Our first step with the child is to bring everything to bear on getting an immediate improvement in the school work. The parents are not directly advised that this is the first step. If they knew it was, they would be discouraged should it fail. (Of course the parents who read this will now know this is an ideal, but will also understand the concomitant problems.) Appropriate tutoring is instituted. The child is brought to an awareness of what he tells himself as he "prepares" for an exam, such as: I'll probably fail; I'd better not take this too seriously; I'll pretend I'm indifferent; My parents will think I'm a fool if I fail; My friends may think I'm a jerk if I study too much; etc. Our purpose in this program is to obtain, if possible, a rapid improvement in school work, even if of minor proportion. If this can be done, the child's self-confidence will be raised considerably. We have found this approach more viable than a passive approach. *This program must be carried out in such a way that the child does not feel the therapist is just another "parent"—always making demands for perfection.* Our reasons for the expanded effort are explained to the child. He is told that our interest is not in better grades but in improved self-

confidence. He is told and shown by example that his status as a human being actually has little to do with his school work, but that his life would certainly be more comfortable and satisfying should he be able to do more efficient work.

With some very passive-aggressive children, an ultra passive, almost passive-aggressive program sometimes works. The therapist does absolutely nothing. The child sees this and begins to criticize the therapist. The therapist gently points out that only the patient can help himself. When the patient then becomes stubbornly silent, the therapist points out his behavior: "You see, this is your typical reaction—the one you use in school. When you feel something is your own personal responsibility, you become passive and demand somebody else do the work. Your way of meeting the threat is to do nothing. Just as you have met the threat of therapy by doing nothing, you have met the threat of school by doing nothing." This approach will not work unless these sequences are *lived out* and *experienced* in the therapy sessions. A premature speech to the child informing him that he meets threat with passivity will be worthless in most cases.

At the slightest hint of setback, an underachiever will further entrench himself in his defensive network. He says to himself: "I tried—I studied—and I still did not do well." He must be shown he is still acting in his typical fashion, that he unreasonably expected and demanded "instant success." He must be shown how he was frightened by the prospect of anything less than complete success and immediately reverted to his typical inefficient maneuvers. It is difficult to get the underachiever past this first stage because to him there is much to risk and little to gain. He must be taught to be content with small gains.

3. The next step in the therapeutic process is more or less standard; a scanning of the life process, with special attention being paid to the factors emphasized in this book. The underachiever is shown how he is made anxious by the feeling of anger, and how his passivity in school is motivated by anger, how he has overly equated his sense of self worth with his ability to be a perfect accomplisher, how he fears failure, how he cannot tolerate aggressively tinged competitiveness, and so forth. Of course these

facets vary with the individual case. Tutoring is meanwhile being given—by someone other than the therapist. The two approaches complement one other. It is important the tutor be a trained psychologist so that he or she can recognize and understand the forces operative in the case. In fact, it is often desirable for the tutor to make certain "interpretations" during the tutoring sessions themselves. Rather than say "You did not seem to prepare today's work too well," the tutor might say: "It seems that something is happening right now to lower your self-confidence." The tutor should complement the general aim of making the child aware of the relation between the quality of his work and the operation of emotional factors. The child's attention should be drawn to this relationship in as concrete a manner as possible. He should be encouraged to realize that conflicted emotional attitudes are causing the difficulty *at the exact instant* of the poor performance. This approach has three major benefits. For one thing, it acknowledges the "truth" of the matter, and forces the child to realize the importance of his inner attitudes. For another thing, it concretizes the nature of the improvement program, and allows the child to see hope for improvement. Dr. Edwin Wagner has pointed out that the feeling of hopelessness is one of the most malignant forces working against the emotionally conflicted individual. The underachiever feels hopeless and helpless in the face of his poor work. He cannot really understand why he does poorly—no matter what he might say to others (e.g., "I'm really not interested," etc.). When he is shown how his emotional attitudes are affecting his performance—and he is shown this in a highly concrete fashion by means of on-the-spot demonstrations —he is shown a road up which he can walk toward success and good feeling. Because the program is made concrete, he can see there is "hope" and that his poor work is not the result of magic and fearsome enemies or bad fate.

A Summary

Our approach with the underachiever begins with a "nonpressure" all-out effort to gain an immediate improvement in school work—even if this improvement is of minor proportion. Tutoring is instituted and the child is urged to pay attention to the thoughts that flash through his mind as he enters a class and before he takes a test. This usually involves ten to fifteen sessions of psychotherapy, and about thirty sessions of tutoring.

If the child is ultra-passive, or if he fears adult manipulation will annihilate his own personality, a more passive approach is employed.

The next phase involves a general scanning of the underachiever's life process, with particular attention to the factors discussed in this book. Tutoring is usually continued through this phase. The tutor should be a trained psychologist, preferably one who has had psychotherapeutic experience, who in on-the-spot demonstrations can draw the child's attention to the relationship between his self-confidence and the quality of his school work. This ideal is difficult to meet, since most tutors lack the training.

If the underachievement has not been of long duration, or is confined to one subject, or is situational and temporary, tutoring alone would probably be indicated. The aim of the tutoring is not to teach "content" alone, but rather to increase the child's self-confidence and to make him feel more comfortable with academic material. The latter aim is accomplished by the tutor's beginning work at a level where the child can begin to experience "success." If after six months it is obvious that the child has made gains as reflected in his performance in the tutoring sessions, but these gains are not being manifested in the school situation, psychotherapy or psychotherapeutically oriented counseling is in order.

Excellent Achievers and Underachievers—Important Similarities: Some Speculations

Erik H. Erikson in his book *Young Man Luther* (New York: Norton, 1962) makes the point of how the very best among us are often but a hairsbreadth different from the very worst. Delicate shifts of balance in mental forces and structures are at work here. Such delicate shifts can determine whether intense emotions will be used for constructive or destructive purposes. Sigmund Freud disturbed the world when he demonstrated some important similarities between the martyr and the gangster. Along much the same lines, underachievers share some important similarities with the best achievers. After reading some of the preceding chapters on the underachiever, the alert reader may have said to himself (correctly) "But this seems true of the good achiever as well!" For example:

Both the underachiever and achiever are overly concerned with achievement, albeit in different ways. (In the remarks to follow, when we say "achiever" we mean the very best achiever.)

Both the achiever and underachiever are very much concerned with parental approval. Both worry a good bit about approval or its absence.

The parents of achievers as well as those of underachievers seem deeply involved and intensely concerned with achievement. (Remember, this does not refer to sociologically induced under-achievement.)

Another interesting phenomenon is the individual who suddenly shifts from underachieving patterns to achieving patterns. (The shift is usually to *compulsive* achieving patterns.)

Excellent achievement can itself spring from many sources, not all of them "healthy." Wilbur Bender (cited by Vernon R. Alden, *Saturday Review,* July 18, 1964) neatly summarizes:

The student who ranks first in his class may be genuinely brilliant or he may be a compulsive worker or the instrument of domineering parents' ambition or a conformist or a self-centered careerist . . . Or he may [focus] . . . on grade-getting as compensation for his inadequacies in other areas, because he lacks other interests or talents or lacks passion and warmth or normal healthy instincts or is afraid of life.

If the remarks to follow were made in the old Scholastic tradition, we would label them "Some Possible Beginning Points for an Elementary Introduction," etc. They are offered in that spirit.

1. Both achievers and underachievers have parents who stress

accomplishment; consequently, children from both groups have overly linked the sense of self worth with the ability to accomplish.

a) A crucial difference seems to rest on the ability of the child to make a relatively conflict-free identification. The achiever has been able to make a conflict-free identification with his achievement-oriented parent(s). The underachiever fears a positive identification would be equivalent to the annihilation of his own personality and hence identifies with the negative traits of his parents, or else forms a "compromise-mixture" solution in which he simultaneously rebels and punishes himeslf for his rebellion, e.g., underachievement. For the underachiever, a parental identification seems to hold much more conflict and fear than for the achiever.

b) The underachiever feels more compelled and commanded to achieve; the achiever works under less stress. The underachiever fears failure to a much greater extent than the achiever. The achiever has a less negative reaction to sarcasm for the same reasons.

c) The underachiever seems to have a *greater* need for individual uniqueness than the achiever. This is perhaps related to "identification threat," i.e., to a desperate need to prove he is "different" or, in analytic terminology, is not emasculated or will not "melt away" in a severe regression.

2. Both the achiever and the underachiever have a strict superego ("conscience").

a) One crucial difference seems to depend on the intensity of the sadistic wrath of the conscience. The underachiever has the more relentless, sadistic conscience. Although one could make many speculations here, there are no clear-cut explanations. The crucial answers may relate to the identification process, but little real research evidence exists in this area.

b) Descriptively, we might say the achiever has a more supportive superego, while the underachiever a more sadistic one. This statement is not meant to be explanatory.

There are many assertions in the literature concerning the

source of the superego's relentless force. The strength and relentlessness of a superego "commandment" makes it seem very much more like an urgent id drive than a mere external command. This is a nonexplanatory explanation, since all energy supposedly derives from the id, later formulations (e.g., conflict-free sphere of ego) notwithstanding. However, assertions such as these open the door to speculations on innate constitutional factors. Psychotherapists have long realized that the neurotic "battle" is not between the self system and an environmental prohibition, but between the self system and an environmental prohibition *armed with the strength of the individual's own drives.* In this sense, the severity of an explicit or implicit command has less to do with the authority and strength of the person who issues it, and more to do with the strength of the drives which reinforce it. A weak king may order a powerful army. There is little factual data in this crucial area. It is often difficult to tell why one individual will have a strict, sadistic superego, and another individual a more lenient one. A straight "environmental" explanation is not convincing.

c) Both the achiever and underachiever are overly interested in pleasing their parents. Again, the identification holds less threat to the achiever, and hence he can "aim to please" with far less ambivalence. The underachiever *tries* to reject his strong need to please his parents, but can only come up with a half-baked or compromise solution, like "good natured" underachievement.

3. The achiever and underachiever both defensively overvalue intelligence.

a) For the many reason cited, the achievers trust their intelligence to a greater degree. Less ambivalence attaches to an "intelligent act."

b) The need for punishment is excessive in the underachieving group.

4. The members of both groups often have an overly close relation with the parents.

a) The degree of unconscious rejection is higher among parents of underachievers.

b) The parent of the achiever is more sure of his adult identity, his intelligence, and his ability to tolerate competition from the child.

c) When there is an almost symbiotic parent-child relation, it is less threatening to the achiever; it is more "open" and accompanied by a conscious recognition of the parental intrusiveness by the achiever; there is less hostility in the closeness of the parent of the achieving child and the child.

d) Members of both groups often feel unloved. For the many reasons cited, this is usually more intense among underachievers.

e) There is a strong desire to be independent in both groups, but the achiever has less need to be "beatnik" since there is less identification threat. He shows his need for independence in intellectual but socially sanctioned areas. Identification with approved parental ideals is far more threatening to the underachiever and consequently the desire to demonstrate independence can reach tremendous proportions. This often leads to a complete disowning of school and educational values.

f) Some (not all) achievers, and hardly any underachievers, can eventually untangle the connection between achievement and the important human object(s) who engendered the achievement motivation. These achievers become "content oriented" and are then more interested in their subjects and less interested in the results or psychological consequences of their achievements. More is implied here than a conflict-free internalization of parental values; this type of unlinking is rare. These individuals develop a genuine fascination with their fields of interest, which is largely unlinked from the ideals, conscious and/or unconscious, of their parents. These "transitions" are relatively rare, and the more important contributions to knowledge come from the members of this select group. The unlinking is especially important if a conflict was largely responsible for vocational choice. In history, there have been few exceptions to this rule; what exceptions exist seem associated with the fields of psychology, philosophy, and religion (where a man can often solve for others what he finds virtually impossible to solve for himself).

37

A Closing Comment
to Parents

How to Proceed If Your Child Is an Underachiever

Should parents have reason to believe their child is under-achieving, individual psychological testing is indicated. It is unwise to have this done by a staff member of the child's school. We do not imply any incompetence on the part of the school staff. But the underachiever's problems are too intimately linked with the very physical reality of the school. Testing done within the physical walls of the school tends to underestimate and otherwise distort the child's true capabilities. A major component of the underachieving child's difficulties is a loss of self-confidence. The child feels particularly unconfident while he is in school. He tenses up; his work suffers. For this reason, it would be difficult to get a good estimate of the child's *potential* capacities from testing done in the physical location of the school. Along similar lines, test scores obtained from confident children are much more likely to reflect true *potential* capacities than are scores obtained from nonconfident children. Remember, we speak of potential capacities. The test scores obtained by the schools reflect usable abilities on all children tested. That is, if a potentially bright, underachieving child takes a test and obtains a mediocre score, that mediocre score successfully mirrors his *current functioning efficiency*. It shows he is doing rather mediocre work. But this child's test battery will likely not reflect his potential capacities —that which he could do were he free of confidence-robbing emotional conflict. On the other hand, when the confident child takes a battery of tests in school, his scores will likely reflect *both* his true potential capacities as well as his usable abilities (of course there should be much less of a gap between these two areas in the confident child as compared to the nonconfident child). Many of these difficulties could be avoided if school systems' psychology staffs were housed away from the actual school buildings, and if everything were done to separate the connection between the psychologist and the school system in the child's mind.

There is another practical reason why individual psychological testing can rarely be done in the school: most schools simply lack enough trained personnel to handle the job. This situation is rapidly changing, but the task is a larger one.

How to Choose Professional Individuals to Work with the Underachieving Child

The first rule is to beware of individuals who advertise services for the underachiever in the common advertising media. Since most professional organizations actively discourage the advertising of professional services, those individuals who do so are obviously at odds with the aims of their own professional organizations. Of course no one could make the blanket statement that any person who advertises his or her services is incompetent.

The best and safest place to apply for help is to any of the following:

1) A college or university. Ask for an out-patient psychological clinic, reading clinic, or educational clinic. Request that a psy-

chologist administer personality tests as well as educational tests.

2) A qualified organization of clinical psychologists. Request the name (usually more than one name is offered) of a psychologist who specializes in the educational problems of children.

3) In out-of-the-way places, the family physician or the local medical society may be able to recommend an appropriate place or person in the vicinity.

4) The school guidance counselor could possibly recommend an appropriate person to administer the individual tests. Too often personal feelings become needlessly involved here, the counselors irrationally feeling they are being avoided in favor of some outsider. Our own personal experiences have been delightfully free of such incidents.

Remember: The individual testing is warranted on the basis of seeking answers to the five questions mentioned at the beginning of the book: What is the child's potential capacity for learning? How is the child actually doing? Is the child, indeed, an underachiever? Why is he an underachiever? What can be done to help him? These questions cannot be answered in the absence of individual test data.

A Note in Closing

Part II has dealt with concrete ways of helping the underachiever become an achiever. As yet, these ways are often time consuming and sometimes expensive. There are no rapid cure-alls. There is no single reason why children do poorly in school. The learning process is complex, involving the organized use of a tremendous number of functions, although conflicted emotional attitudes are most frequently responsible for a breakdown in this process. The efficiency with which a person learns is not only based on intelligence, but on the entire life process. Therefore it is perhaps not unreasonable that the corrective procedure be time consuming and complex. A good many of the attitudes by means of which the child experiences and acts in the world have to be examined, clarified, and ironed out. If this book can help some families to work through these problems, we will be pleased.

About the Authors

BARRY BRICKLIN, Ph.D., is a research assistant professor of psychiatry (psychology) at the Hahnemann Medical College of Philadelphia. He was formerly an instructor in psychiatry (psychology), and an associate in the Department of Psychiatry at the Jefferson Medical College of Philadelphia. He has been a consultant to the Walter Reed Army Hospital Research Center, to the E. I. duPont de Nemours Co., and to the Kimberton Farms School. Dr. Bricklin is past president of the Philadelphia Society for Projective Techniques, and past president of the Philadelphia Society of Clinical Psychologists. He is co-author of a book on a new projective test, and among others has published articles on prognosis in schizophrenia, marital compatibility, the psychology of affiliation, the intercultural use of the Rorschach, and Ethiopian children. Dr. Bricklin has worked with underachieving children as a psychodiagnostician and psychotherapist, in private practice and in institutional settings.

PATRICIA M. BRICKLIN, Ph.D., is psychological consultant to the Valley Day School for children with learning and adjustment problems. Formerly, she was a consultant to the Bucks County Public Schools. Dr. Bricklin has lectured in psychology at Temple University and was supervisor of the diagnostic division of the university's reading clinic. She has been a consultant to the learning disability clinic at Jefferson Medical College, has conducted workshops on reading disabilities in public and private schools, and taught in-service reading courses for elementary and high school teachers. For five years she taught children with severe learning and adjustment problems at the Matthews School, of Baltimore, Maryland, and Fort Washington, Pennsylvania.

Dr. Patricia Bricklin is past president of the Philadelphia Society for Projective Techniques. She has published articles on the diagnosis and treatment of children with reading disabilities and has frequently spoken on these issues at the Temple University Reading Institutes and at meetings of the International Reading Association.

Among the things on which she has cooperated in producing with her husband are this book and two sons, Brian and Scott.

The Bricklins are hosts of the popular WCAU radio (CBS, Philadelphia) show, "The Bricklins," a program predominantly on child psychology. They are heard daily, Mondays through Fridays, 11:35 to 12 noon.